NORTH CAROLINA
COMMUNICABLE DISEASE LAW

JILL D. MOORE

2017

 UNC
SCHOOL OF GOVERNMENT

The School of Government at the University of North Carolina at Chapel Hill works to improve the lives of North Carolinians by engaging in practical scholarship that helps public officials and citizens understand and improve state and local government. Established in 1931 as the Institute of Government, the School provides educational, advisory, and research services for state and local governments. The School of Government is also home to a nationally ranked Master of Public Administration program, the North Carolina Judicial College, and specialized centers focused on community and economic development, information technology, and environmental finance.

As the largest university-based local government training, advisory, and research organization in the United States, the School of Government offers up to 200 courses, webinars, and specialized conferences for more than 12,000 public officials each year. In addition, faculty members annually publish approximately 50 books, manuals, reports, articles, bulletins, and other print and online content related to state and local government. The School also produces the *Daily Bulletin Online* each day the General Assembly is in session, reporting on activities for members of the legislature and others who need to follow the course of legislation.

Operating support for the School of Government's programs and activities comes from many sources, including state appropriations, local government membership dues, private contributions, publication sales, course fees, and service contracts.

Visit sog.unc.edu or call 919.966.5381 for more information on the School's courses, publications, programs, and services.

Michael R. Smith, Dean
Thomas H. Thornburg, Senior Associate Dean
Frayda S. Bluestein, Associate Dean for Faculty Development
Johnny Burleson, Associate Dean for Development
Michael Vollmer, Associate Dean for Administration
Linda H. Weiner, Associate Dean for Operations
Janet Holston, Director of Strategy and Innovation

FACULTY

Whitney Afonso
Trey Allen
Gregory S. Allison
David N. Ammons
Ann M. Anderson
Maureen Berner
Mark F. Botts
Anita R. Brown-Graham
Peg Carlson
Leisha DeHart-Davis
Shea Riggsbee Denning
Sara DePasquale
James C. Drennan
Richard D. Ducker
Robert L. Farb
Norma Houston

Cheryl Daniels Howell
Jeffrey A. Hughes
Willow S. Jacobson
Robert P. Joyce
Diane M. Juffras
Dona G. Lewandowski
Adam Lovelady
James M. Markham
Christopher B. McLaughlin
Kara A. Millonzi
Jill D. Moore
Jonathan Q. Morgan
Ricardo S. Morse
C. Tyler Mulligan
Kimberly L. Nelson
David W. Owens

LaToya B. Powell
William C. Rivenbark
Dale J. Roenigk
John Rubin
Jessica Smith
Meredith Smith
Carl W. Stenberg III
John B. Stephens
Charles Szypszak
Shannon H. Tufts
Vaughn Mamlin Upshaw
Aimee N. Wall
Jeffrey B. Welty
Richard B. Whisnant

Contents

Preface / vii

Part 1

Overview of the Main Components of North Carolina Communicable Disease Law / 1

Chapter 1

Introduction / 3
  Defining "Communicable Disease" and "Communicable Condition" / 5
  Role of the Public Health System in Communicable Disease Control / 6
    Roles of State Officials and Agencies / 6
    Roles of Local Officials and Agencies / 7
    Role of Federal Officials and Agencies / 8

Chapter 2

Detecting Communicable Disease in the Population / 9
  Communicable Disease Reporting in North Carolina / 10
    Routine Communicable Disease Reporting / 10
    Non-Routine Reporting: Temporary Orders to Report / 14
    Immunity from Liability for Reporters / 16
  Special Categories of Reports / 16
    Health Care–Associated Infections / 16
    Reports Related to Nuclear, Biological, or Chemical Terrorism / 17
  Population Surveillance / 20

Chapter 3

Controlling the Spread of Disease / 23
  Investigating Cases and Outbreaks / 23
    Access to Information for Investigations / 24
    Contact Tracing and Partner Notification / 25

Communicable Disease Control Measures / 26

Identifying the Required Communicable Disease Control Measures / 27

Control Measures for Emerging Illnesses / 27

Isolation and Quarantine / 29

Communicable Disease Outbreaks Caused by Terrorism / 29

Chapter 4

Enforcement: Remedies for Communicable Disease Law Violations / 31

Criminal Enforcement: Misdemeanor / 31

Initiating a Misdemeanor Charge / 32

Trial and Sentencing / 35

Special Considerations for Arrest and Detention / 36

Civil Enforcement: Injunction / 37

Procedure for Using This Remedy / 37

Using This Remedy for Communicable Disease Law Violations / 39

Chapter 5

Communicable Disease and Confidentiality Law / 41

The HIPAA Privacy Rule and the State Communicable Disease Confidentiality Law / 42

Overview and Comparison of the Two Laws / 42

Overview of Relevant Provisions of the HIPAA Privacy Rule / 43

Overview of the State Communicable Disease Confidentiality Law / 44

Disclosure of Information That Is Not Identifiable / 47

Obtaining Communicable Disease Information for Public Health Purposes / 47

Obtaining Information through Communicable Disease Reports / 47

Obtaining Information Relevant to a Case or an Outbreak Investigation / 48

Public Health Officials' Obligation to Maintain the Confidentiality of Communicable Disease Information / 49

HIPAA and Communicable Disease Information Held by Public Health Agencies / 49

State Communicable Disease Confidentiality Law and Public Health Activities / 50

Disclosing Information about Communicable Disease to the Public / 51

Public Disclosure with the Individual's Written Authorization / 51

Public Disclosure When the Information Is Necessary to Protect the Public Health and the Disclosure Is Made in Accordance with the North Carolina Communicable Disease Control Rules / 52

Public Disclosure When the Information That Is Released Is for Statistical Purposes Only and Cannot Be Used to Identify an Individual / 53

Part 2

Special Topics in North Carolina Communicable Disease Law / 55

Chapter 6

Isolation and Quarantine / 57
  Definition of Isolation and Quarantine / 57
  Ordering Isolation or Quarantine / 60
    Authority to Order Isolation or Quarantine / 60
    Decision to Order Isolation or Quarantine / 63
    How Isolation or Quarantine Is Ordered / 63
    Duration of Isolation or Quarantine Orders / 65
  Due Process Rights of Isolated or Quarantined Persons / 67

Chapter 7

Bloodborne Pathogen Exposures / 69
  Two Sources of Regulation: OSHA Standards and North Carolina Rules / 70
    The Universal Precautions Approach / 70
    Other Similarities and Differences / 71
    Exposure Incidents / 73
    Significant Risk of Transmission / 74
    Required Follow-Up / 75
    Refusal of Required Tests / 79

Chapter 8

Bioterrorism and Public Health / 81
  Public Health Threats Caused by Terrorism / 82
  State Health Director Powers over Property / 83
    Tests for Contamination / 83
    Closing or Evacuating Property for Evacuations / 83
    Order to Abate a Public Health Threat / 83
  Powers over Persons and Animals / 84
    Tests or Examinations / 84
    Limitations on Freedom of Movement, Action, or Access / 84

Appendixes

Appendix 1: Communicable Disease Law Glossary / 89

Appendix 2: Index of North Carolina Communicable Disease Statutes and Rules, by Topic / 93

Appendix 3: Selected North Carolina General Statutes / 97

Appendix 4: Selected Internet Sites Addressing Communicable Disease Control / 125

Preface

This book provides an introduction to the law of communicable disease control in North Carolina. It is divided into two parts. Part 1 addresses the core topics in the legal structure for communicable disease control: detecting communicable disease in the population through surveillance and disease reporting laws, investigating communicable disease cases and outbreaks, controlling communicable disease, enforcing communicable disease laws using public health legal remedies, and the interaction of confidentiality laws with public health agencies' communicable disease control activities. Part 2 takes a more in-depth look at three special topics. The first two—isolation and quarantine authorities and bloodborne pathogen exposures—represent specialized communicable disease control measures that deserve deeper attention than they receive in the general chapter on controlling communicable disease. The third topic, public health and bioterrorism, describes laws that would operate in tandem with communicable disease laws in the event of bioterrorism involving a communicable disease agent.

As the title indicates, the book is intended to be an overview of key topics. It does not attempt to cover every subtopic or answer every question that may arise. The book is supplemented by materials on my North Carolina public health law website, ncphlaw.unc.edu. Follow the link to "Legal Information by Topic" and select the topic "Communicable Disease Control" for links to blog posts, bulletins, and frequently asked questions about some of the topics in this book.

This work has benefitted tremendously from many years of close work with North Carolina state and local public health officials and attorneys. The constant contact between the SOG and the public officials we serve is a pleasure and an honor, and it makes my work better. I am especially grateful to Chris Hoke and John Barkley, who helped me understand the history and practical context of the issues underlying the statutory framework for public health law, and to my SOG colleague Aimee Wall, who has been my sounding board on more occasions than I can count. I am fortunate to have such talented individuals as colleagues and friends.

Jill D. Moore, MPH, JD
Associate Professor of Public Law and Government
The University of North Carolina at Chapel Hill
September 2016

Part 1

Overview of the Main Components of North Carolina Communicable Disease Law

Chapter 1

Introduction

Perhaps the most outstanding feature of the health work during the year 1918 was the epidemic of influenza. The epidemic began early in October and caused in October alone 6,056 deaths...

BIENNIAL REPORT OF THE NORTH CAROLINA STATE BOARD OF HEALTH, VOL. 18 (1919–1920)[1]

In mid-year of 1948, North Carolina was visited by the most widespread epidemic of poliomyelitis in its history, and one of the worst ever recorded in the United States. During this epidemic, there were 2,517 cases reported to the State Board of Health and 147 deaths.

DR. J.W.R. NORTON, ANNUAL REPORT OF THE NORTH CAROLINA BOARD OF HEALTH TO CONJOINT SESSION STATE MEDICAL SOCIETY, MAY 11, 1949[2]

North Carolina Department of Health and Human Services public health officials and staff from local health departments are now investigating 19 cases of measles in Stokes, Orange and Polk counties as part of an outbreak that was first reported in mid-April. Since the outbreak began, state and local public health authorities have notified more than 1,000 people in Stokes, Forsyth, Guilford, Orange, Polk and Chatham counties who may have been exposed to the disease.

NORTH CAROLINA DEPARTMENT OF HEALTH AND HUMAN SERVICES PRESS RELEASE, April 30, 2013[3]

---

1. Report available through the UNC Libraries North Carolina Health History Digital Collection, http://archives.hsl.unc.edu/nchh/nchh-02/nchh-02-018.pdf.

2. Report available through the UNC Libraries North Carolina Health History Digital Collection, http://archives.hsl.unc.edu/nchh/nchh-02/nchh-02-033.pdf.

3. Press Release, N.C. Department of Health and Human Services, State Health Officials Continue Investigation and Control of Statewide Measles Outbreak (Apr. 30, 2013), https://www2.ncdhhs.gov/pressrel/2013/2013-04-30_measles_outbreak.htm.

Preventing and controlling the spread of communicable disease is one of the core activities of public health systems throughout the world and has been for centuries. It is an area that has seen great success. Infectious disease control and the related topic of immunization were identified by the Centers for Disease Control and Prevention (CDC) as two of the "Ten Great Public Health Achievements of the 20th Century."[4] And yet communicable disease never completely goes away. Smallpox was vanquished at about the same time Ebola emerged. By the 1980s, fear of polio was a distant memory for the United States, but fear of HIV/AIDS was new and strong. The twenty-first century has already seen the emergence of SARS, novel influenzas, and new mosquito-borne illnesses and the re-emergence of measles in the United Kingdom. Communicable disease is perennial, and there is every reason to believe that it will remain a perennial concern of public health systems.

Law provides part of the infrastructure that allows public health systems to detect and respond to communicable diseases and conditions. In North Carolina, the legal framework for communicable disease control includes provisions for the following:

- *Detection* of communicable diseases and conditions within the population
- *Investigation* of cases and outbreaks by public health officials
- *Communicable disease control measures* that specify the steps individuals, health care providers, public health officials, or others must take to control the spread of disease
- *Legal remedies* to enforce communicable disease laws
- Access to and protection of *confidential information* that is necessary to carry out communicable disease activities

The legal framework is composed largely of state statutes and administrative regulations. This book contains several appendixes to help the reader navigate the framework and understand its specialized vocabulary. Appendix 1 is a brief glossary of communicable disease terms that have statutory or regulatory definitions. Appendix 2 provides an index, organized by topic, of the statutes and the regulations that are associated with

---

4. Centers for Disease Control and Prevention, *Ten Great Public Health Achievements in the 20th Century*, www.cdc.gov/about/history/tengpha.htm.

them. The relevant state statutes are collected and reprinted in Appendix 3. Appendix 4 provides a list of Internet sites that have additional information about communicable disease control or communicable disease law.

Defining "Communicable Disease" and "Communicable Condition"

What constitutes a disease or condition that is subject to the communicable disease laws? In our day-to-day communications, we may use the term "communicable disease" to refer only to illnesses that are contagious from person to person. In North Carolina, however, the legal definition of communicable disease captures those types of illnesses but also goes further, to pick up a number of illnesses that may be transmitted from one person to another via an agent rather than directly. Communicable disease is defined by a North Carolina statute as an illness caused by an infectious agent—usually a virus or bacterium—that can be transmitted from person to person, from an animal to a person, through an intermediate host or vector, or through the inanimate environment.[5] This definition captures a wide range of diseases that may be transmitted from one person to another through casual contact (such as measles), intimate contact (such as gonorrhea), or even from mother to child during pregnancy (such as congenital syphilis). It also captures diseases that are spread through other means, such as foodborne illnesses, sickness caused by contaminated water, or disease caused by a vector such as a tick or mosquito.

A person has a "communicable condition" if the person has been infected with a communicable agent but does not have symptoms of disease.[6] Infection with HIV is an example of a communicable condition, as it describes a condition that has not yet progressed to the disease state.

North Carolina's communicable disease laws apply to both communicable diseases and communicable conditions.

---

5. N.C. GEN. STAT. (hereinafter G.S.) § 130A-2(1c). This definition is substantially similar to the definition of "communicable disease" found in *A Dictionary of Epidemiology* (Oxford University Press, 5th edition 2008), at 46.
6. G.S. 130A-2(1b).

Role of the Public Health System in Communicable Disease Control

All levels of government—federal, state, and local—have a role in communicable disease control. However, primary responsibility is borne by state and local governments.

In North Carolina, responsibility for controlling communicable disease is shared by state and local public health officials. Much of the work occurs at the local level, but much of the legal framework is at the state level. In an outbreak, state officials typically take the lead in developing and coordinating the response. State statutes and rules authorize and define the scope of local public health officials' communicable disease activities. State-provided materials—such as case definitions, control measures, guidance documents, or templates for isolation or quarantine orders—are important documents for local public health officials to consult to ensure that their actions during an outbreak are consistent with both state communicable disease laws and current best practice recommendations.

Roles of State Officials and Agencies

At the state level, the North Carolina Commission for Public Health makes communicable disease control rules.[7] The state secretary of health and human services is charged with overseeing communicable disease prevention and control.[8] The secretary appoints the state health director, a North Carolina–licensed physician who performs duties and exercises authority delegated by the secretary.[9] The state health director also has multiple specific duties in the communicable disease realm. Among other things, he or she has the authority to examine patient records pertaining to communicable diseases[10] and to order isolation or quarantine in appropriate circumstances.[11] The state health director has additional authorities when there is a health threat that may have been caused by terrorism using nuclear, biological, or chemical agents.[12]

---

7. G.S. 130A-147.
8. G.S. 130A-5(2).
9. G.S. 130A-3.
10. G.S. 130A-144(b).
11. G.S. 130A-145.
12. G.S. 130A-476. Because some such agents could cause communicable diseases, it is possible there could be an event in which the communicable disease laws

North Carolina also has a state epidemiologist, who is a medical doctor with an advanced degree in epidemiology. Among other duties, the state epidemiologist oversees the work of the Communicable Disease Branch, a component of the Division of Public Health within the state Department of Health and Human Services. The Communicable Disease Branch receives reports of cases of communicable diseases, coordinates and conducts disease surveillance and disease investigation activities, coordinates the public health response to outbreaks, provides assistance and support to local public health agencies responding to communicable disease, and provides public information about communicable diseases.[13] The State Laboratory of Public Health provides laboratory services that support the diagnosis of communicable diseases and conditions.[14]

Roles of Local Officials and Agencies

At the local level, the directors of local health departments must receive reports of communicable diseases and conditions, investigate reported cases, ensure that communicable disease control measures prescribed by the Commission for Public Health have been explained to the appropriate parties, disseminate public health information, and advise local health officials about public health matters. Local health directors also are empowered to examine patient records pertaining to communicable disease and to exercise quarantine and isolation authority.[15]

In some counties, local public health services are provided through a consolidated human services agency (CHSA). When a county creates a CHSA and gives it the responsibility for local public health services, the director of the CHSA acquires the powers and duties of a local health director—including all of the duties related to communicable disease control.

---

and public health bioterrorism laws would both be applicable. For more information about North Carolina public health law and bioterrorism, see Chapter 8.

13. The Communicable Disease Branch is part of the Division of Public Health's Epidemiology Section. For more information about the branch, see its website at http://epi.publichealth.nc.gov/cd/.

14. The State Laboratory of Public Health is also a component of the Division of Public Health. For more information about the state lab, see its website at http://slph.ncpublichealth.com/.

15. *See* G.S. 130A-135 through -139 (communicable disease reports); 130A-144 (communicable disease investigation and control); 130A-145 (isolation and quarantine authority); 130A-41 (general powers and duties of local health directors).

However, the communicable disease–related duties may be delegated to another person.[16] If the CHSA director does not have the education and experience that is required to be a local health director, the CHSA director must appoint an individual who does,[17] and it is customary to delegate local health director powers and duties to that person.

Role of Federal Officials and Agencies

The federal government certainly has a stake in the control of communicable diseases within the United States, but its legal role is limited, and in practice its role is usually supportive and advisory. Federal laws are focused on preventing the introduction of communicable disease into the United States and on preventing interstate spread of disease.[18]

The greater role for the federal government is carried out by the Centers for Disease Control and Prevention (CDC), which develops case definitions for identifying communicable disease and guidelines for managing communicable disease. CDC guidelines serve as the basis for the communicable disease control measures that are required by North Carolina law.[19]

The federal government also provides technical assistance and in some instances sends personnel to assist states and local governments with their disease control efforts. The CDC also conducts research and public health surveillance—activities that provide the foundation for communicable disease detection and response.

---

16. G.S. 153A-77(e) ("Except as otherwise provided by law, the human services director or designee shall have the same powers and duties as ... a local health director ..."); *see also* G.S. 130A-43(c) (a consolidated human services director has the powers and duties of a local health director provided by G.S. 130A-41); 130A-6 (authorizing a public official with authority under G.S. Chapter 130A to delegate that authority to another person).

17. G.S. 153A-77(e)(9). The appointee must meet qualifications specified in G.S. 130A-40(a). The county manager must approve the appointment.

18. For more information about these laws, see Chapter 6.

19. N.C. ADMIN. CODE (hereinafter N.C.A.C.) tit. 10A, ch. 41A, § .0103(a). Also see "Communicable Disease Control Measures" in Chapter 3.

Chapter 2

Detecting Communicable Disease in the Population

In order to control the spread of communicable disease in a population, public health officials must first detect it. Public health disease surveillance, "the ongoing, systematic collection, analysis and interpretation of the who, what, where, when and how of disease case occurrence in a population,"[1] is carried out by state and federal agencies. Communicable disease reporting is at the foundation of effective public health surveillance systems, and it starts at the local level, when a health care provider or other person detects a case of a reportable disease.

Every state has one or more laws that require health care providers to report communicable diseases and conditions that have been designated *reportable* to local or state public health officials. The laws vary from state to state on matters including who must report and which diseases or conditions must be reported. They are subject to change over time, especially as new illnesses emerge.[2] Communicable disease reports typically include individually identifiable information.

States, in turn, voluntarily provide information to the Centers for Disease Control and Prevention (CDC) about diseases designated *notifiable*. The CDC prepares a national list of notifiable diseases, but these too may vary by state, as not every state requires reports of the diseases on the CDC's notifiable disease list. Notifiable disease reports that are made to the CDC do not include personal identifiers.[3]

---

1. N.C. Division of Public Health, Communicable Disease Surveillance and Reporting, http://epi.publichealth.nc.gov/cd/report.html.

2. It is more common for a disease to be added to the reportable list than to be removed. In North Carolina, the number of reportable diseases and conditions increased significantly over a 20-year period, from 58 in 1996 to 74 in 2016. The 1996 version of the rules is on file with the author.

3. *See* https://wwwn.cdc.gov/nndss/.

This chapter reviews North Carolina's communicable disease reporting laws and briefly describes the surveillance systems operated by North Carolina and the CDC.

Communicable Disease Reporting in North Carolina

North Carolina law provides for both mandatory and voluntary communicable disease reporting, and both routine and non-routine reporting occasions. There are also special provisions in state law for reporting health care–associated infections and conditions that may have been caused by terrorism using nuclear, biological, or chemical agents.

Routine Communicable Disease Reporting

State laws require physicians and certain others to routinely report more than 70 communicable diseases and conditions. The list of reportable communicable diseases is adopted as a rule by the Commission for Public Health and is published in the North Carolina Administrative Code.[4] It includes tuberculosis, many vaccine-preventable diseases, laboratory-confirmed HIV, hepatitis, sexually transmitted infections, foodborne diseases, illnesses caused by contaminated water, mosquito- and tick-borne illnesses, novel influenzas, and diseases that may be caused by bioterrorism.

Physicians

A physician must make a report when the physician has reason to suspect that a person who has consulted him or her professionally—in other words, a patient—has a disease or condition that has been designated reportable.[5] The North Carolina Division of Public Health provides case definitions to assist physicians in knowing when a report is required.[6] For most diseases and conditions, a physician is not required to wait for a diagnosis to be

---

4. N.C. ADMIN. CODE (hereinafter N.C.A.C.) tit. 10A, ch. 41A, § .0101(a). The North Carolina Administrative Code is available at http://reports.oah.state.nc.us/ncac.asp. The general rule is that a physician should report either knowledge or suspicion of a reportable disease in a patient.

5. N.C. GEN. STAT. (hereinafter G.S.) § 130A-135.

6. See the state's online communicable disease manual, available at http://epi.publichealth.nc.gov/cd/lhds/manuals/cd/toc.html.

confirmed by laboratory or other tests. However, HIV is not reportable until it is confirmed.

Reports must be made to the local health department[7] within time frames prescribed by the Commission for Public Health. Some diseases and conditions must be reported immediately, some within 24 hours, and some within seven days.[8] The information to be reported is prescribed by the administrative rules that establish the list of reportable diseases and the communicable disease measures. The information that must be reported always includes the patient's name and the disease or condition the patient has (or is suspected of having). Additional information may be required as well, depending on the disease or condition.[9]

The patient's permission is not required to make the report. On the conrary, the physician must make a report when the reporting law requires it, even if the patient objects. Public health officials who receive the information are required to keep the information confidential and may not release identifiable information about communicable diseases except as specifically allowed by a state statute.[10]

The reporting law gives the duty to report to physicians and doesn't mention other types of health care providers, but if another practitioner—such as a nurse—suspects a reportable communicable disease in a patient, that practitioner should notify the supervising physician to ensure the report is made.

---

7. The statute states that reports must be made to the local health director. In practice, it is likely that a communicable disease nurse or other appropriate health department staff member would receive the report.

8. 10A N.C.A.C. 41A. 0101(a).

9. 10A N.C.A.C. 41A. 0102(a).

10. G.S. 130A-143. The statute permits public health officials to release identifiable information in order to control the spread of communicable disease; however, any such release must be made in accordance with the North Carolina communicable disease control rules. *See also* Act-Up Triangle v. Comm'n for Health Servs., 345 N.C. 699 (1997) (acknowledging the confidential nature of HIV information and upholding the state's HIV reporting requirement only after concluding that the state communicable disease confidentiality law was sufficient to guard against unauthorized public disclosure of the information).

Other Reporters

In addition to physicians, other entities and people who are required to make communicable disease reports include laboratories, operators of restaurants, and school principals and child care operators. These reporters' legal duties, described below, are not exactly the same as the duties imposed on physicians.

Persons in Charge of Laboratories

Laboratories must report positive tests for tuberculosis, gonorrhea, syphilis, and other lab test results that are specified in an administrative rule.[11] The list of reportable test results is related to the list of diseases and conditions that are reportable by physicians—capturing the same general set of vaccine-preventable diseases, bloodborne diseases, sexually transmitted infections, foodborne diseases, and vector-borne illnesses—but it is tailored to reflect the specific laboratory findings that indicate those diseases are present. Laboratory reports to public health officials may be made electronically via the North Carolina Electronic Disease Surveillance System (NC EDSS).

Operators of Restaurants or Other Food and Drink Establishments

An operator of a restaurant or other food and drink establishment is required to report only when the operator has reason to suspect an outbreak of a foodborne illness associated with the operator's establishment or when the operator has reason to suspect that a food handler at the establishment has a foodborne illness or condition. A state administrative rule specifies the diseases and conditions that restaurant operators must report.[12] Because it is focused on foodborne illness, the list is shorter than the list of diseases and conditions that physicians must report. In 2016, the list consisted of 17 illnesses, including hepatitis A; diarrheal illnesses such as shigellosis, botulism and other causes of "food poisoning"; cholera; and non-cholera vibrio infections. Required reports must be made to the local health department.

School Principals and Child Care Operators

State law directs school principals and child care operators to make a report to the local health department when a person in the school or child care

---

11. G.S. 130A-139; 10A N.C.A.C. 41A .0101(c).
12. G.S. 130A-138; 10A N.C.A.C. 41A .0102(b) & (c).

facility has any reportable disease.[13] However, if the report is about a student, a school principal's ability to report may be limited by the federal Family Educational Rights and Privacy Act,[14] which permits such reports without prior parental consent only if the illness creates a health or safety emergency in the school.[15]

Medical Facilities

Medical facilities are authorized, but not required, to make a report to the local health department when a patient in the facility is reasonably suspected of having a reportable communicable disease or condition.[16] This report is voluntary and may appear redundant, because any physicians who work in the facilities are already required to make reports. However, this provides another route to get the information if a physician's report is not made for some reason. In the absence of this law expressly permitting voluntary reports, the facilities might not be able to make such reports due to confidentiality laws.[17]

Local Health Directors

Local health directors are the recipients of communicable disease reports, but they are also mandated reporters. First, local health directors are responsible for forwarding all of the reports they receive to the state Division of Public Health. In most cases, this may be done electronically, via the NC EDSS.[18] However, there are administrative rules that require telephone

---

13. G.S. 130A-136.

14. 20 U.S.C. § 1232g; 34 C.F.R. pt. 99.

15. 34 C.F.R. § 99.31 (10) (authorizing disclosures without prior consent in connection with health or safety emergencies as described in Section 99.36); 34 C.F.R. § 99.36 (authorizing disclosure when an educational agency or institution, considering the totality of the circumstances, determines that there is an articulable and significant threat to the health or safety of the student or other individuals). For a fuller discussion of this issue, see U.S. Department of Health & Human Services and U.S. Department of Education, *Joint Guidance on the Application of the Family Educational Rights and Privacy Act (FERPA) and the Health Insurance Portability and Accountability Act of 1996 (HIPAA) to Student Health Records* (Nov. 2008), www2.ed.gov/policy/gen/guid/fpco/doc/ferpa-hipaa-guidance.pdf.

16. G.S. 130A-137.

17. For more information, see Chapter 5.

18. G.S. 130A-40; *see also* 10A N.C.A.C. 41A .0103(a)(3) (describing the methods and time frames for forwarding reports to the state). For a brief description of the history and features of the NC EDSS, see http://epi.publichealth.nc.gov/cd/lhds/manuals/cd/ncedss/NCEDSS.pdf.

reports of certain findings.[19] Second, if a local health department receives a report about a person who is a resident of a county served by a different local health department, the local health director who received the report must report the case and any laboratory findings to the local health director for the county where the person resides.[20]

The local health director must also make reports to the Division of Public Health in the event of an outbreak. If the outbreak involves a reportable disease, the local health director must submit a written report of the outbreak investigation, its findings, and the actions taken to control the outbreak within 30 days. If the outbreak involves a disease or condition that is not reportable, the health director must give appropriate control measures for the disease and inform the Division of Public Health about the circumstances of the outbreak within seven days.[21]

Non-Routine Reporting: Temporary Orders to Report

A state statute authorizes the state health director to issue a temporary order requiring health care providers to report symptoms, diseases, conditions, trends in the use of health care services, or other health-related information that may indicate the existence of a communicable disease or a communicable condition that threatens the public health.[22] This authority is limited to the state health director. Local health directors may not issue such orders.

The purpose of this statute is to permit the detection of new or emerging communicable conditions that are either not yet understood well enough to be identifiable diseases or syndromes (thus, the authority to require reports of symptoms or health care use) or that are recognized diseases or conditions that have not yet been placed on the reportable list. This authority was

---

19. 10A N.C.A.C. 41A .0103(a)(3)(A) requires the local health director to make telephone reports of all cases of primary, secondary, and early latent syphilis to the regional office of the HIV/STD Prevention and Care Branch within 24 hours of either making the diagnosis at the health department or receiving a report of the diagnosis from a physician. 10A N.C.A.C. 41A .0103(a)(3)(B) requires the local health director to make a telephone report of all reactive syphilis serologies of pregnant women and certain others to the regional office of the Division of Public Health within 24 hours of receipt.

20. G.S. 130A-140.

21. 10A N.C.A.C. 41A .0103(c).

22. G.S. 130A-141.1.

Figure 2.1.   State Health Director's Temporary Order

TEMPORARY ORDER

ZIKA VIRUS INFECTION

Pursuant to G.S. 130A-141.1, the State Health Director hereby issues a TEMPORARY ORDER requiring physicians licensed to practice medicine in this State and laboratories operating in this State to report suspected or confirmed Zika virus infections. This order is based upon the findings that reports of Zika virus infection are necessary for surveillance of a communicable disease that presents a danger to the public health. The report is required to be made within 24 hours when Zika virus infection is reasonably suspected to exist. The physician shall make the report to the local health director of the county or district in which the patient resides. The local health director shall report the infection to the Division of Public Health within 24 hours. The laboratory shall make the report directly to the Division of Public Health. This order is effective February 1, 2016 and expires in 90 days.

Randall Williams, MD
State Health Director

first provided to the state health director in legislation adopted in 2004[23] in the immediate aftermath of 2003's severe acute respiratory syndrome (SARS) epidemic, when it became clear that existing reporting requirements might allow initial cases of conditions such as SARS to slip through the cracks. Since its adoption, the authority has been exercised several times. Figure 2.1 provides an example of a state health director's temporary order.

The state health director's order must specify which health care providers must report,[24] what information must be reported, and the period of

---

23. S.L. 2004-80 (S 582).

24. The temporary order may require any of the following persons to report: "a physician licensed to practice medicine in North Carolina or a person who is licensed, certified, or credentialed to practice or provide health care services, including, but not limited to, pharmacists, dentists, physician assistants, registered nurses, licensed practical nurses, advanced practice nurses, chiropractors, respiratory care therapists, and emergency medical technicians." *See* G.S. 130A-141.1(b) (incorporating by reference the definition of "health care provider" in G.S. 130A-476(g)).

time for which reporting is required. The period of time specified in the order may not exceed 90 days. If a longer period is necessary to protect the public health, the Commission for Public Health may adopt rules to continue the reporting requirement.[25]

Immunity from Liability for Reporters

A person who makes any of the routine or non-routine reports described above is immune from any liability that might otherwise be imposed under state law for making the report.[26] Reporters nevertheless sometimes worry about liability under other laws, such as HIPAA.[27] However, the HIPAA Privacy Rule specifically permits disclosures of protected health information to public health authorities pursuant to laws requiring or authorizing reports about disease.[28] Additional information about the interaction between HIPAA and state communicable disease laws is in Chapter 5.

Special Categories of Reports

Health Care–Associated Infections

Since 2012, North Carolina hospitals have been required to participate in a surveillance system designed to monitor health care–associated infections.[29] Health care–associated infections are, in essence, infections that patients acquire from the environment in the facility itself. More specifically, they are defined as infections caused by infectious agents or toxins when there is no evidence that the patient was already infected before being admitted to the health care setting.[30] Hospitals must make monthly reports of such infections electronically through the National Healthcare Safety

---

25. G.S. 130A-141.1(a).

26. G.S. 130A-142.

27. Health Insurance Portability and Accountability Act, Pub. L. 104-191, 110 Stat. 1936 (1996). Subtitle F of Title II of the act, known as the administrative simplification provisions, authorized the adoption of federal regulations to protect the privacy and security of health information.

28. 45 C.F.R. § 164.512(a) & (b).

29. G.S. 130A-150.

30. The administrative rules define a health care–associated infection as "a localized or systemic condition in the patient resulting from an adverse reaction to the presence of an infectious agent(s) or its toxin(s) with no evidence that the

Network.[31] The infections to be reported are identified in rules adopted by the federal Centers for Medicare and Medicaid Services (CMS). The CMS rules are incorporated by reference into North Carolina's communicable disease rules.[32]

Reports Related to Nuclear, Biological, or Chemical Terrorism

Acts of bioterrorism have resulted in outbreaks of communicable disease in the United States. Letters containing anthrax sickened 23 individuals and killed five in the fall of 2001. The anthrax letters may be the best-known example of bioterrorism causing communicable disease, but it is not the only instance. Another occurred in 1984, when a religious cult intentionally contaminated salad bars at 10 Oregon restaurants with salmonella in order to sway a local election.[33]

The potential for bioterrorist acts to result in illness, perhaps including communicable diseases, prompted changes in North Carolina law in 2002. State law now provides for both mandatory and voluntary reporting of conditions that could indicate that a bioterrorist act has occurred.[34] Those reporting requirements are described below. For additional information about public health and bioterrorism, see Chapter 8.

Mandatory Reports Pursuant to State Health Director's Temporary Order

The state health director may issue a temporary order requiring certain reports when the director determines that reports are necessary to the conduct of an investigation or surveillance of an illness, condition, or health hazard that may have been caused by terrorism using nuclear, chemical, or biological agents.[35] Note that this authority is limited to the state health director. Local health directors may not issue such orders.

The temporary order may require health care providers to report symptoms, diseases, conditions, trends in use of health care services, or other

---

infection was present or incubating when the patient was admitted to the health care setting." 10A N.C.A.C. 41A .0106(a)(3).

31. For more information about the National Healthcare Safety Network, see http://www.cdc.gov/nhsn/.

32. 10A N.C.A.C. 41A .0106.

33. *See* Jill D. Moore, *Unnatural Disasters: Bioterrorism and the Role of Government*, POPULAR GOV'T, Summer 2002, at 4.

34. G.S. 130A-476.

35. G.S. 130A-476(b).

health-related information. The order must specify which health care providers are required to report,[36] what information must be reported, and the period of time for which reporting is required (not to exceed 90 days). If a period of longer than 90 days is necessary to protect the public health, the Commission for Public Health may adopt rules to continue the reporting requirement.

At the time of this writing, no temporary orders have been issued under the authority of this statute—all of the state health director temporary orders of recent years have been under the authority of the communicable disease temporary order statute described above. A temporary order issued under the authority of this statute would supplement but not replace the usual requirements for reporting communicable diseases. Physicians and other mandatory reporters would still be required to comply with routine communicable disease reporting laws while the temporary order was in effect.

A person who makes a report pursuant to the state health director's temporary order is immune from any liability that might otherwise arise under North Carolina law.[37] Reporters nevertheless sometimes worry about liability under other laws, such as HIPAA. However, the HIPAA Privacy Rule specifically permits disclosures of protected health information to public health authorities pursuant to laws requiring or authorizing reports about disease.[38]

---

36. The temporary order may require any of the following persons to report: "a physician licensed to practice medicine in North Carolina or a person who is licensed, certified, or credentialed to practice or provide health care services, including, but not limited to, pharmacists, dentists, physician assistants, registered nurses, licensed practical nurses, advanced practice nurses, chiropractors, respiratory care therapists, and emergency medical technicians." *See* G.S. 130A-476(g).

37. G.S. 130A-476(d).

38. 45 C.F.R. § 164.512(a) & (b).

Voluntary Reports of Events That May Indicate Bioterrorism

North Carolina's public health bioterrorism laws also authorize voluntary reports to public health officials in certain circumstances. Health care providers,[39] people in charge of health care facilities,[40] and units of state or local government may make voluntary reports of events that may indicate an illness, condition, or other health hazard that may have been caused by terrorism using nuclear, chemical, or biological agents. The events that may be reported include unusual types or numbers of symptoms or illnesses, unusual trends in health care visits, or unusual trends in prescriptions or purchase of over-the-counter pharmaceuticals. The information may be reported to either the state health director or a local health director.[41]

A person or entity that makes a report under this provision must refrain from disclosing personally identifiable information, if practicable.[42] The reference to what is "practicable" seems to recognize the possibility that some circumstances might require that a person's identity be disclosed. However, if information that might identify an individual is not necessary, it should not be disclosed. A person who makes a voluntary report in good faith is immune from liability that might otherwise arise under state law. A person who fails to make a report is also immune from liability, unless the person is a health care provider who had actual knowledge that a condition or illness was caused by the use of a nuclear, biological, or chemical weapon of mass destruction.[43]

---

39. For purposes of this statute, "health care provider" is defined to include "a physician licensed to practice medicine in North Carolina or a person who is licensed, certified, or credentialed to practice or provide health care services, including, but not limited to, pharmacists, dentists, physician assistants, registered nurses, licensed practical nurses, advanced practice nurses, chiropractors, respiratory care therapists, and emergency medical technicians." G.S. 130A-476(g)(1).

40. For purposes of this statute, "health care facility" is defined to include "hospitals, skilled nursing facilities, intermediate care facilities, psychiatric facilities, rehabilitation facilities, home health agencies, ambulatory surgical facilities, or any other health care related facility, whether publicly or privately owned." G.S. 130A-476(g)(2).

41. G.S. 130A-476(a).

42. G.S. 130A-476(a).

43. *Id.*

If a communicable disease is believed to have been caused by bioterrorism, both the usual communicable disease reporting requirements and the requirements that are specific to bioterrorism apply.

Population Surveillance

In North Carolina, communicable disease reports from clinicians and laboratories are entered into the NC EDSS.[44] This information feeds into the federal National Electronic Disease Surveillance System (NEDSS) that is maintained by the CDC for nationwide surveillance of diseases and conditions of public health significance.

Communicable disease surveillance is also conducted through an electronic system called the North Carolina Disease Event Tracking and Epidemiologic Collection Tool (NC DETECT). This system receives data daily from hospital emergency departments and the Carolinas Poison Center and allows public health officials to detect information that may indicate that a communicable disease or other public health threat is present in the population, perhaps before it is otherwise recognized or reported.[45]

North Carolina also participates in a surveillance program that is specifically focused on the epidemics of flu that the United States experiences each year. The North Carolina Influenza Sentinel Surveillance Program is part of a national network of public and private health care providers who assist public health officials in monitoring the extent of flu outbreaks and the strains of influenza viruses that are circulating. Health care providers and facilities that participate in the sentinel network make weekly reports to public health agencies. The reports include the total number of patient visits for the week, as well as the number of patients who had influenza-like

---

44. More information about the NC EDSS system is available at http://epi.public health.nc.gov/cd/about/ncedss.html.

45. G.S. 130A-480, enacted in 2004, requires hospital emergency departments to participate in a syndromic surveillance system, designed to detect public health threats resulting from bioterrorism or communicable disease outbreaks, by providing data electronically to the Division of Public Health. NC DETECT is the system that receives the data. A state administrative rule prescribes the data that must be submitted. 10A N.C.A.C. 41A .0105. For more information about NC DETECT, see www.ncdetect.org/.

illness (ILI).[46] From this, public health officials can calculate the percentage of visits to sentinel providers that are the result of ILI. Sentinel providers also collect lab samples on a portion of the patients with ILI. Those samples are sent to the State Laboratory for Public Health, which tests the samples to determine whether influenza virus is present and, if so, the strain of the virus.[47] During the United States influenza season, which is approximately October through May each year, weekly flu surveillance reports are prepared in North Carolina and made available to the public through the state's flu website, flu.nc.gov. The methods of monitoring flu activity in North Carolina cannot capture every case that occurs in the state, so the numbers reported represent only a small portion of the number of actual cases that are present during any given week. However, they provide information about the types of flu that are circulating and allow public health officials to advise clinicians and the public about the nature and extent of influenza activity in the state.

---

46. The program defines ILI as a fever of 100 degrees Fahrenheit or higher, accompanied by a cough or sore throat.

47. For more information about North Carolina's flu sentinel program, see www.epi.state.nc.us/epi/gcdc/flusentsurv.html.

Chapter 3

Controlling the Spread of Disease

Once a communicable disease or condition is detected, public health officials may take various actions to control its effects on the infected individual and to guard against its spread in the population. North Carolina laws address how public health officials investigate cases and outbreaks of communicable disease and how they determine the control measures to apply to prevent or reduce the spread of disease.

Investigating Cases and Outbreaks

Local health directors in North Carolina are required by law to investigate cases and outbreaks of communicable diseases and conditions.[1] They are assisted in this effort by state and regional public health officials. Among other things, the local health director's investigation must identify the persons for whom communicable disease control measures are required. If control measures are required, the director must ensure that the measures are explained to the proper parties and that the parties comply.[2]

The state Communicable Disease Branch has a number of manuals that go into detail about the step-by-step investigation process for different communicable diseases. Most of the manuals include a section with a title that refers to either disease investigation or investigation steps. The general communicable disease manual includes investigation steps for most of the reportable communicable diseases. There are also disease-specific manuals for hepatitis B, rabies control, sexually transmitted diseases, and tuberculosis. The manuals may be accessed online through the Division

---

1. N.C. GEN. STAT. (hereinafter G.S.) § 130A-144(a); N.C. ADMIN. CODE (hereinafter N.C.A.C.) tit. 10A, ch. 41A, § .0103(a) & (b).
2. 10A N.C.A.C. 41A .0103.

of Public Health website.[3] In the event of an emerging illness that is not addressed in a manual, the division typically issues guidance documents that provide case definitions, identify control measures, and address the disease investigation steps.

Access to Information for Investigations

In the course of a disease investigation, public health officials will obtain information from a number of sources. These sources include, but are not limited to, the infected person, if possible; other exposed persons, if they are known; health care providers involved in the diagnosis and treatment of the infected persons; and, potentially, business owners or others. Specific state laws authorize public health officials to obtain even confidential information when certain conditions are met.

Physicians, persons in charge of medical facilities, and persons in charge of laboratories are required by law to permit public health officials to examine, review, and obtain a copy of medical records pertaining to the diagnosis, treatment, or prevention of communicable diseases or conditions. Other persons may be required to make other types of records available as well.[4] For example, in the investigation of a foodborne illness, public health officials may request the names of individuals who dined at a particular food establishment (gathered from credit card receipts). A public health official requesting information must show proper identification.[5]

A similar law requires health care providers and persons in charge of health care facilities or laboratories to permit public health officials to examine, review, and obtain a copy of records containing information that is protected by HIPAA or another confidentiality law when the information is necessary for a public health investigation into an illness or public health threat that may have been caused by terrorism using nuclear, chemical, or biological agents.[6]

---

3. N.C. Division of Public Health, *Communicable Disease Manual* (2012), http://epi.publichealth.nc.gov/cd/lhds/manuals/cd/toc.html.

4. G.S. 130A-144(b).

5. The law specifies that the state health director or a local health director shall have access to the information upon request and proper identification. However, the person making the request may be a person with delegated authority from the state or local health director. *See* G.S. 130A-6 (authorizing a public official with authority under G.S. Chapter 130A to delegate that authority to another person).

6. G.S. 130A-476(c).

Persons who permit the examination, review, or copying of records in accordance with these laws are immune from civil or criminal liability that might otherwise be imposed.[7] Health care providers may still worry about liability under other laws, such as HIPAA. However, the HIPAA Privacy Rule specifically permits disclosures of protected health information to public health authorities pursuant to laws requiring or authorizing reports about disease.[8] For more information on confidentiality laws and communicable disease activities, see Chapter 5.

Contact Tracing and Partner Notification

"Contact tracing" is the term used to describe the public health activity of identifying individuals who may have been exposed to someone who is infected with a communicable disease or condition. For infections that are transmitted sexually, partner notification programs include both identifying contacts and ensuring that exposed persons are notified either by the partners who exposed them or by public health officials.

When contact tracing or partner notification is a communicable disease control measure, individuals are required by North Carolina law to comply with it.[9] North Carolina administrative rules expressly require individuals who are infected with certain communicable diseases or conditions to identify or notify contacts or partners, which may include household or other contacts, sexual partners, or needle-sharing partners.[10] The Division of Public Health conducts a partner notification program to assist in notifying and counseling the partners of individuals with HIV.[11]

Contact tracing may also be a required control measure for other communicable diseases. The following section on communicable disease control measures contains more information about how required communicable disease control measures are determined.

---

7. G.S. 130A-144(c) (communicable disease investigations); 130A-476(d) (investigations related to terrorism).

8. 45 C.F.R. § 164.512(a) & (b).

9. G.S. 130A-144(f) (requiring all persons to comply with communicable disease control measures established by the Commission for Public Health).

10. See 10A N.C.A.C. 41A .0202 (HIV); .0203 (hepatitis B); .0204(c) (syphilis, lymphogranuloma venereum, granuloma inguinale, chancroid); .0205 (tuberculosis); .0214 (hepatitis C).

11. 10A N.C.A.C. 41A .0202(13).

Communicable Disease Control Measures

North Carolina law authorizes the Commission for Public Health to adopt communicable disease control measures and requires all persons to comply with them.[12] Failure to comply is a violation of public health laws that may be enforced through the use of public health remedies.[13] The commission's rules are published in Title 10A, Subchapter 41A, of the North Carolina Administrative Code. The term *communicable disease control measures* is not defined in state law, but it has the meaning common sense would suggest: measures or steps that are taken to control the spread of a communicable disease.

Local health directors are responsible for ensuring that communicable disease measures are "given"[14]—which in practice often simply means ensuring that people who may spread the disease are informed about the required control measures. The term could also mean instructing other persons or entities to take particular steps to prevent the spread of disease.

While most of North Carolina's body of communicable disease control law addresses the authorities and responsibilities of the public health system, portions create legal obligations for private parties as well. Physicians, in particular, have several important legal duties. Physicians must

- report communicable diseases and conditions to the local health director,[15]
- instruct individuals with communicable diseases and conditions in the disease control measures that are required by law,[16] and
- cooperate with communicable disease investigations by making records and information available to public health officials who properly request them.[17]

---

12. G.S. 130A-144.

13. G.S. 130A-18 (injunction); 130A-25 (misdemeanor). For more information on enforcing communicable disease laws, see Chapter 4.

14. G.S. 130A-144(e).

15. G.S. 130A-135.

16. 10A N.C.A.C. 41A .0210.

17. G.S. 130A-144(b).

Identifying the Required Communicable Disease Control Measures

The Commission for Public Health has adopted rules specifying the communicable disease control measures for only a few communicable diseases and conditions: HIV, hepatitis B and C, sexually transmitted diseases, tuberculosis, smallpox/vaccinia, and SARS.[18] For other communicable diseases, the required control measures are derived from guidelines and recommended actions published by the federal Centers for Disease Control and Prevention (CDC), or if no such materials are available, from the guidelines and recommendations that appear in the *Control of Communicable Diseases Manual*, a publication of the American Public Health Association (APHA).[19] Both the CDC documents and the APHA manual are incorporated by reference into the commission's rules.[20]

The commission also has prescribed general principles to be followed in applying the manual's control measures and in devising control measures for communicable diseases and conditions for which there are no specific control measures. Among other things, those principles state that control measures must be reasonably expected to decrease the risk of transmission and must be consistent with recent scientific and public health information.[21]

Control Measures for Emerging Illnesses

"Emerging illness" is a term used to describe two different types of diseases: those that are entirely new to a population, as HIV was in the early 1980s, or known diseases that have begun to increase in frequency or geographic spread, as West Nile virus did in the early 2000s. When an emerging illness approaches or appears in North Carolina, the relevant disease control measures will likely be derived from the documents incorporated by reference into the administrative rules—that is, the guidelines and recommended actions published by the CDC. In the absence of CDC guidelines, control measures may be derived from APHA's *Control of Communicable*

---

18. 10A N.C.A.C. 41A .0202–.0205, .0208, .0213, .0214.

19. D.L. HEYMANN, ED., CONTROL OF COMMUNICABLE DISEASES MANUAL (20th ed. 2014). Hard copy or digital subscription versions may be ordered at www.apha.org/ccdm.

20. 10A N.C.A.C. 41A .0201(a).

21. 10A N.C.A.C. 41A .0201(b).

Diseases Manual, if it addresses the disease in question,[22] or devised in accordance with the principles in 10A N.C.A.C. 41A .0201(a). Control measures for emerging illnesses typically are determined by the state Division of Public Health and disseminated to local health departments.

By incorporating the CDC documents into North Carolina's communicable disease rules, the Commission for Public Health has attempted to ensure that the control measures required by state law are aligned with up-to-date scientific understanding about emerging illnesses. However, this presents a challenge: it is not unusual for control measures for an emerging illness to change as understanding about the illness develops. This makes sense, as there may be many unknowns: In what ways does the disease spread, and how readily? How severe is it? Are existing treatments effective, or is something new required? Are certain people more susceptible than others? The answers to all of these questions are relevant to developing appropriate control measures, and as answers emerge the control measures may change. This means, however, that public health officials must be diligent in keeping up with the changes and effective in communicating those changes to the public—tasks that are neither simple nor easy. For example, at the outset of the H1N1 pandemic in 2009, CDC guidance advised school closure if any student or staff member developed the flu. But very shortly thereafter, the CDC rescinded that guidance and replaced it with recommendations for schools that did not include closure in most circumstances. This created confusion and posed a significant communication challenge for public health and school officials throughout the United States—including in North Carolina, where a school closure occurred right before the guidance changed.

Public health officials also must keep people who are subject to control measures apprised of any changes. It is important to keep a record of what the control measures are on the day they are given, just in case they change. If a public health official must give control measures based on electronic guidance posted on the CDC or DPH website, the official should save or print a copy of the guidance document, date it, and keep careful records that clearly identify the date of the CDC document the official relied on when the control measures were given. This could be important if the official later must justify the control measures that were given on the particular date.

---

22. 10A N.C.A.C. 41A .0201(a).

Isolation and Quarantine

Isolation and quarantine are communicable disease control measures. In common parlance, isolation and quarantine are usually assumed to mean physical separation of an individual from the public. North Carolina law on isolation and quarantine authority incorporates the concept of physical separation, but it also goes beyond that to serve as a kind of enforcement tool for all of the communicable disease control measures, including those that do not involve physical separation from the public. The North Carolina law is sufficiently complex to warrant its own chapter in this book. Chapter 6 discusses North Carolina isolation and quarantine law.

Communicable Disease Outbreaks Caused by Terrorism

It is possible that a communicable disease outbreak could be caused by an act of bioterrorism.[23] If this were to occur, all the usual communicable disease laws would still apply, including the authority to order isolation or quarantine. However, some additional legal authorities become effective when the state health director reasonably suspects that a public health threat may exist and may have been caused by a terrorist incident using nuclear, biological, or chemical agents.[24] These additional authorities may be exercised only by the state health director. The additional authorities that are most likely to apply in a communicable disease outbreak that may have been caused by terrorism are as follows:

- The state health director may require any person or animal to submit to examinations and tests to determine possible exposure to nuclear, biological, or chemical agents.
- The state health director may limit the freedom of movement or action of a person or animal that is contaminated with, or reasonably suspected of being contaminated with, a nuclear, biological, or chemical agent that may be conveyed to others. This sounds like isolation or quarantine authority, but it is different because it applies

---

23. Public health authority during a terrorist event is discussed in more detail in Chapter 8.

24. G.S. 130A-475.

to persons or animals who are *contaminated* rather than to persons who are infected or exposed to a communicable disease.[25]

- The state health director may limit access by any person or animal to an area or facility that is housing persons or animals whose freedom of movement or action has been limited because they are contaminated with a nuclear, biological or chemical agent. The director may also limit access by any person or animal to an area or facility that is contaminated with such an agent.

All of these authorities may be exercised only when and for so long as a public health threat may exist, all other reasonable means for correcting the problem have been exhausted, and no less-restrictive alternative exists. There is a 30-day limitation on the period of time a person's freedom of movement or access may be limited that parallels the 30-day limitation on isolation or quarantine orders restricting freedom of movement or access. A person who is substantially affected by the state health director's order may institute an action for review of the order in superior court. If the state health director determines that additional time is needed, the director may institute an action in superior court for an additional 30-day period (and may seek additional 30-day extensions as needed).

---

25. The distinction may not matter much in practice when the agent is one that causes communicable disease, such as anthrax spores. A person who is contaminated with such an agent probably has also been exposed to communicable disease, so quarantine authority would also apply. See Chapter 6 for more information about quarantine authority.

Chapter 4

Enforcement: Remedies for Communicable Disease Law Violations

All persons shall comply with control measures, including submission to examinations and tests, prescribed by the Commission [for Public Health] . . .

NORTH CAROLINA GENERAL STATUTES § 130A-144(f)

What happens when someone doesn't comply with communicable disease laws? There are two public health remedies that may be used to enforce the state laws: one criminal and one civil. On the criminal side, a person who violates any of North Carolina's communicable disease statutes or rules may be charged with a Class 1 misdemeanor. The laws may also be enforced through a civil action—a local health director may file an action for injunctive relief in a superior court. While any violation of the North Carolina communicable disease laws may be enforced using these remedies, in practice they are most commonly employed to address violations of communicable disease control measures or violations of isolation or quarantine orders.

Criminal Enforcement: Misdemeanor

A person may be charged with a Class 1 misdemeanor for violating any of North Carolina's public health statutes or rules except those pertaining to smoking.[1] In the communicable disease context, a misdemeanor charge may be brought when

---

1. N.C. GEN. STAT. (hereinafter G.S.) § 130A-25(a). This statute does not prescribe the classification for the misdemeanor, so under G.S. 14-3 it is classified as Class 1.

- a person fails to comply with communicable disease control measures established by the Commission for Public Health in violation of Section 130A-144(f) of the North Carolina General Statutes (hereinafter G.S.),[2] or
- a person violates an isolation or quarantine order issued by a local health director or the state health director pursuant to G.S. 130A-145.

Initiating a Misdemeanor Charge

To initiate a misdemeanor charge, a judicial official (ordinarily a magistrate) must determine that there is probable cause that a crime has been committed. Public health officials and employees are likely to be the people involved in assembling the information that the magistrate needs to make this decision. They will need to provide information about the applicable laws as well as the facts that establish the violation. Magistrates are, of course, familiar with criminal law and know how to charge a misdemeanor. However, communicable disease law violations are uncommon compared to other crimes that the judicial system encounters, so instituting this particular charge is probably not a routine procedure for any given judicial official. Further, the explanation of exactly which law has been violated is complicated, because it involves not only the two statutes cited above but also the rules in the North Carolina Administrative Code that specify communicable disease control measures. It also may involve other documents from which control measures have been derived, such as CDC guidance documents that have been incorporated by reference into the rules. The following examples illustrate this complexity:

> *Violation of HIV control measures.* Mr. Smith was diagnosed with HIV in 2010. At that time, he was informed that he is required to comply with the HIV control measures established by North Carolina law. He signed a document that listed the control measures and included a statement affirming that he understood the control measures and his obligation to comply with them. The control measures listed in

---

2. G.S. 130A-144(f) requires all persons to comply with the control measures the Commission for Public Health establishes. The specific control measure(s) that are required are disease-specific and are set out in Title 10A, Subchapter 41A, §§ .0201–.0214 of the North Carolina Administrative Code (hereinafter N.C.A.C.). For more information about how control measures are determined, see "Communicable Disease Control Measures" in Chapter 3.

the document included notifying sexual partners of his HIV infection and using condoms during sexual intercourse. In 2016, two persons newly diagnosed with HIV identify Mr. Smith as a sexual partner and tell public health officials that he did not tell them he had HIV and did not use condoms during sexual intercourse. If these allegations are true, Mr. Smith has violated G.S. 130A-144(f), the statute that requires compliance with control measures, and 10A N.C.A.C. 41A .0202, the rule that specifies the HIV control measures that were listed on the document Mr. Smith signed. G.S. 130A-25(a) makes these violations a misdemeanor.

Violation of rubella control measures. Ms. Williams works as a server in a restaurant. Shortly after a trip abroad, she becomes ill and is diagnosed with rubella (German measles).[3] The county communicable disease nurse informs Ms. Williams that she is required to be isolated for seven days after the onset of her rash to protect others, especially pregnant women, as the disease poses a particular risk to fetuses. Ms. Williams is only mildly ill and does not need to be hospitalized, so she is instructed to remain at home. She agrees and signs a document to that effect. However, the communicable disease nurse sees Ms. Williams working in the restaurant the very next day. In order to demonstrate that Ms. Williams violated G.S. 130A-144(f), public health officials would need to show that she violated control measures established by the Commission for Public Health. The commission's rules do not contain a specific section for rubella, but they incorporate by reference CDC guidelines and recommended actions for communicable disease control.[4] The CDC guidelines on rubella

---

3. G.S. 130A-152 requires children to be vaccinated against rubella. The disease has been eliminated from the United States, meaning it no longer originates here, but cases may be imported by travelers to areas where it is still endemic. Because it is unlikely that a vaccinated person would acquire rubella, the person in this hypothetical likely was not vaccinated—perhaps because she qualified for a medical or religious exemption to the vaccine requirements. *See* G.S. 130A-156; 130A-157. A person with an exemption from vaccination is *not* exempt from the obligation to comply with communicable disease control measures if he or she acquires the vaccine-preventable disease.

4. 10A N.C.A.C. 41A .0201(a).

state that patients should be isolated for seven days after rash onset.[5] Therefore, the allegations against Ms. Williams are that she violated G.S. 130A-144(f) and 10A N.C.A.C. 41A .0201. These violations are made a misdemeanor by G.S. 130A-25(a).

Because of this complexity and the relative rarity of these types of cases, a public health official who wants to initiate a misdemeanor charge against a person who violates communicable disease laws should assemble the relevant laws, rules, and guidance documents establishing the control measures, along with evidence to support probable cause that the person has violated the control measures.[6] If the individual was subject to an isolation or quarantine order, the order will be an important part of the evidence. The public health official should be prepared to explain the authority for the order and whether the order restricted the individual's freedom of movement, freedom of access, or freedom of action.[7]

If the magistrate finds probable cause to believe that the communicable disease laws have been violated, the magistrate may charge the individual with a misdemeanor and issue a criminal summons or a warrant for the person's arrest.[8]

---

5. H. McLean et al., *Rubella*, Ch. 14 *in* Manual for the Surveillance of Vaccine-Preventable Diseases (Apr. 1, 2014), www.cdc.gov/vaccines/pubs/surv-manual/chpt14-rubella.html.

6. In a case involving a communicable disease law violation, the evidence required to support probable cause is likely to be confidential under one or more laws. The applicable confidentiality laws expressly allow disclosure of information to judicial officials in order to enforce the communicable disease laws; however, public health and judicial officials should be aware that the information is confidential and should take appropriate steps to protect the information from public disclosure. See "Overview of the State Communicable Disease Confidentiality Law" in Chapter 5 for more information.

7. Chapter 6 describes the isolation and quarantine authorities and explains the terms *freedom of movement, freedom of access,* and *freedom of action.*

8. A criminal summons (www.nccourts.org/Forms/Documents/13.pdf) orders the defendant to appear in court on a certain date to answer to the charges, but the person is not arrested. An arrest warrant (www.nccourts.org/Forms/Documents/1.pdf) requires law enforcement to arrest and detain the defendant until conditions for pretrial release are set.

Trial and Sentencing

The case is heard in the district court of the county where the offense occurred.[9] If the person is convicted, he or she may appeal to superior court for trial de novo.[10] Notice of appeal must be given within 10 days of the conviction in district court.

If a person is convicted of violating communicable disease control measures or violating an isolation or quarantine order, North Carolina's structured sentencing laws do not apply and the person may be sentenced for a period of up to two years.[11] The sentence must be served in one of several facilities specified in state law.[12] A person sentenced under this provision may not be released before the term of imprisonment is completed unless a district court determines that the person's release would not endanger the public health. Before reaching such a conclusion, the court must receive recommendations from the medical consultant for the confinement facility, in consultation with the local health director for the person's county of residence.[13]

---

9. G.S. 15A-131(a).

10. *Trial de novo* means that the case is re-tried anew. The superior court is not limited to reviewing the district court's decision to determine whether there were errors of law; it re-hears the case completely, including any disputes about facts as well as applicable laws.

11. G.S. 130A-25(b).

12. *Id.* The specific facilities are McCain Hospital, the North Carolina Correctional Center for Women, or another confinement facility designated for this purpose by the state secretary of public safety after consultation with the state health director. The purpose of this requirement is to ensure that the defendant serves the sentence in a facility that is equipped to address the defendant's medical needs and protect against the further spread of disease within the confinement facility.

13. G.S. 130A-25(c). This procedure is typically followed for persons who are convicted of violating tuberculosis control measures and sentenced to two years. Ordinarily, if the convicted person complies with medical treatment for tuberculosis while incarcerated, he or she will recover and no longer pose a threat to the public health after six to nine months. The *North Carolina Tuberculosis Control Policy Manual* addresses the procedure for incarceration and release of a tuberculosis law violator in Chapter IV, Part Q, epi.publichealth.nc.gov/cd/lhds/manuals/tb/Chapter_IV_2015.pdf.

Special Considerations for Arrest and Detention

If a local health director decides to pursue criminal enforcement of the communicable disease laws, the director should consider whether following the normal procedures for arresting and detaining the person creates a risk of spreading disease to others. This could be an issue when a defendant has (or has been exposed to) a disease that can spread through a type of contact that is likely to occur during arrest or detention. For example, this concern would likely exist for a defendant who violates a quarantine order related to a novel influenza or a disease such as Ebola. However, it would not be a concern for a person charged with violating control measures for a disease or condition that requires intimate contact, such as HIV or syphilis.

To address these concerns, 2002 legislation amended North Carolina's criminal procedure laws to allow for arrests and detentions that minimize the exposure of others to the arrested person.[14] A law enforcement officer who arrests an individual for violating an isolation or quarantine order *that limits freedom of movement or freedom of access* may detain the person in an area designated by the state health director or a local health director until the individual's first appearance before a judicial official.[15] At the first appearance, the judicial official must consider whether the person poses a threat to the health and safety of others.[16] If the judicial official determines by clear and convincing evidence that the person does pose a threat, the official must deny pretrial release and order the person to be confined in an area that the official designates after receiving recommendations from the state health director or local health director. The burden to produce sufficient evidence to support the determination that the person poses a threat is on the health director. These provisions do not apply to isolation or quarantine orders limiting *freedom of action.*[17]

---

14. S.L. 2002-179 (H 1508).

15. G.S. 15A-401(b)(4).

16. G.S. 15A-534.5.

17. The distinction between orders limiting freedom of movement, orders limiting freedom of access, and orders limiting freedom of action is explained in Chapter 6.

Civil Enforcement: Injunction

The communicable disease statutes and rules may also be enforced through a civil action. A local health director or the state health director may request an injunction from the superior court in the county in which a violation of the communicable disease laws occurred.[18]

If a local health director wishes to pursue this remedy, it is essential to engage the health department's attorney in the process. At the outset, the attorney can help the director evaluate whether it is an appropriate course of action in the specific case. If it is, the attorney will be needed to prepare the appropriate documents and take the steps required to get the matter before the court.

Procedure for Using This Remedy

The following list summarizes the general process and steps that the health director may anticipate.[19] However, an attorney with litigation experience will be familiar with the process of initiating a civil action and may not follow these steps precisely. A local health director should be aware that this action requires adherence to the Rules of Civil Procedure and should not substitute this description for the advice of the department's attorney.

1. To initiate this remedy, the health department's attorney must prepare a civil complaint. There is no official form for a basic civil complaint, but an attorney with litigation experience will be able to produce this document. The text of the complaint should include at least all of the following:

   - The county of residence of the person who has violated the public health statute or rule (the defendant)
   - A statement of the facts establishing that the person has violated the public health statute or rule
   - A recitation of the statute or rule that the person has violated
   - The county where the violation was committed

---

18. G.S. 130A-18.

19. I am indebted to my colleague Ann Anderson, who provided a draft of this section. Among other things, Professor Anderson specializes in the law of civil procedure.

- A statement of the local health director's authority to bring the action for injunctive relief
- A request for injunctive relief

2. The health department's attorney must file the complaint with the clerk of superior court in the county where the violation occurred or where the defendant resides.

3. The local health department's attorney may then move for a temporary restraining order (TRO) from a superior court judge at the time the complaint is filed. Requesting a TRO is the method for obtaining quick action under G.S. 130A-18. Otherwise, the case will proceed under the normal time frames in the Rules of Civil Procedure. Those time frames require serving the complaint on the public health law violator (which may take several days) and allowing the violator 30 or more days to file a response. The process of having a hearing on a TRO varies from courthouse to courthouse. In some areas, the clerk of court's office may be able to assist the attorney in making arrangements for an ex parte hearing on the TRO. The procedure and standards for obtaining a TRO are found in Rule 65 of the Rules of Civil Procedure.[20] They must be strictly followed for the TRO to be valid. Rule 65 requires that a TRO include specific written findings by the court, and the order must be filed with the clerk of court as soon as it is granted. For this reason, it may also be a good idea to have a template TRO prepared in advance if the health director anticipates using this civil remedy.

4. If a TRO is granted, it is effective for 10 days (which may be extended by the court for good cause shown). Once the TRO is filed with the clerk, the health department's attorney should serve it upon the defendant as soon as possible. If the defendant violates the TRO, the local health department's attorney may make a motion to enforce the TRO. This typically involves seeking an order of civil contempt. The procedure and standards for holding someone in civil contempt are governed by G.S. 5A-21 through -23. The procedures include a five-day notice requirement for the violator

---

20. G.S. 1A-1, Rule 65.

"unless good cause is shown."[21] The remedy for civil contempt is imprisonment.[22]

5. The action may proceed to a hearing for a preliminary injunction (a short-term order that may be issued while the action is pending) or a permanent injunction (the court's final order to the individual to cease the violation of the law). The local health director must continue to work with the department's attorney to pursue these orders.

Using This Remedy for Communicable Disease Law Violations

This remedy may be used to enforce the communicable disease laws. In the communicable disease context, it is most likely to be used when

- a person fails to comply with the communicable disease control measures established by the Commission for Public Health, in violation of G.S. 130A-144(f); or
- a person violates an isolation or quarantine order issued by a local health director or the state health director pursuant to G.S. 130A-145.

Two special considerations when using this remedy in the communicable disease context are discussed below.

Timeliness

If a person violates a communicable disease control measure or an isolation or quarantine order, quick action may be needed to protect the public health. For this reason, it is a good idea to have template documents drafted in advance. A local health director may wish to work with his or her attorney to develop a template complaint and a template TRO.

Detaining a Person Who Violates a TRO or an Injunction

A person who violates a court's order could potentially be held in civil contempt. The remedy for civil contempt is imprisonment as long as the contempt continues. Ordinarily, imprisonment is in the local jail. However, this may be problematic in the communicable disease context, especially if the disease is one that spreads without intimate contact. If the local

---

21. G.S. 5A-23(a).

22. G.S. 5A-21. A person who is found in civil contempt may be imprisoned as long as the contempt continues, subject to limitations in the statute.

jail is not equipped to keep the person confined in a manner that is safe for all involved—including the jail staff and the other inmates—the local health department should be prepared to identify and request from the court an alternative location for the person to be detained. This may also require working closely with the local sheriff or jail administrator to obtain a "safekeeper" order,[23] allowing the defendant to be transferred from the local jail to another facility.

---

23. G.S. 162-39 authorizes a sheriff to seek an order from a superior court judge to transfer a local inmate to another local jail or a state prison facility when necessary for the safety of the inmate or the security of the local jail. An inmate who is transferred under this provision is called a "safekeeper."

Chapter 5

Communicable Disease and Confidentiality Law

Information about communicable diseases or conditions is health information. There are several laws that protect the confidentiality of health information. The best known and arguably most significant is the HIPAA Privacy Rule,[1] a federal law. There are also a number of state laws addressing medical confidentiality in North Carolina, including laws that are particular to certain professionals[2] or specific to different types of health care facilities.[3] However, the most significant state law in this context is Section 130A-143 of the North Carolina General Statutes (hereinafter G.S.), a law that is specific to information and records that identify a person who has or may have a reportable communicable disease (hereinafter the state communicable disease confidentiality law).

A full treatment of all of these confidentiality laws is well beyond the scope of this chapter. Indeed, a full treatment of every issue that arises just in the communicable disease realm is beyond the scope of anything purporting to be an overview. However, most practical questions that public health agencies have about the confidentiality of communicable disease information can be answered by considering the HIPAA Privacy Rule in

---

1. 45 C.F.R. pts. 160 & 164. HIPAA stands for the Health Insurance Portability and Accountability Act of 1996, Pub. L. 104-191. Among other things, it authorized the federal Department of Health and Human Services to adopt regulations protecting the privacy of individually identifiable health information.

2. *See, e.g.,* N.C. GEN. STAT. (hereinafter G.S.) § 8-53 (creating physician–patient privilege and articulating a general rule of confidentiality for medical records and information); 8-53.13 (nurse–patient privilege); 143-518 (confidentiality of information acquired by emergency medical services providers).

3. *See, e.g.,* G.S. 130A-12 (making patient information maintained by local health departments confidential); 131E-97 (confidentiality of patient medical and financial records maintained by hospitals generally).

conjunction with the state communicable disease confidentiality law. This chapter describes those two laws and discusses their application to two key issues: how public health officials may obtain confidential communicable disease information for public health purposes and public health officials' obligation to maintain the confidentiality of the communicable disease information they acquire. It concludes with a section addressing the disclosure of information about communicable disease to the public.

The HIPAA Privacy Rule and the State Communicable Disease Confidentiality Law

Overview and Comparison of the Two Laws

Both HIPAA and the state communicable disease confidentiality law affect public health communicable disease control activities. They both allow public health officials to acquire, use, and disclose the information that is needed to carry out those activities. However, they also establish limits on the use and disclosure of individually identifiable information in order to protect the privacy of the individuals to whom the information pertains. The combination of permissions (allowing the acquisition, use, and disclosure) and restrictions (limits on uses and disclosures) thus strikes a balance between individuals' interest in privacy and the public's interest in controlling the spread of disease.[4]

The two laws are different in several significant ways. First, there is a difference in the entities to which they apply. The HIPAA Privacy Rule applies only to "covered entities"—a term that captures most health care providers, as well as some (but not all) public health programs.[5] In contrast, the state

---

4. *See* Act-Up Triangle v. Comm'n for Health Servs., 345 N.C. 699 (1997) (upholding the state's HIV reporting requirement after concluding that the state communicable disease confidentiality law was sufficient to guard against unauthorized public disclosure of the information).

5. Every local public health agency in North Carolina is either a stand-alone HIPAA-covered entity or part of a HIPAA-covered entity. The state Department of Health and Human Services is also covered by HIPAA. However, the HIPAA Privacy Rule may not cover all of a covered entity's functions and activities if the entity has determined that it is a *hybrid entity* and has excluded some of its programs, functions, or activities from HIPAA coverage. A full treatment of this complex subject is beyond the scope of this section. For a description of the hybrid

communicable disease confidentiality law applies to *any* public or private entity that has information or records that identify a person who has or may have a reportable communicable disease.

Second, the laws differ in the information they cover. The HIPAA Privacy Rule applies to "protected health information" (PHI), defined as individually identifiable health information that relates to an individual's health status or condition, the provision of health care to the individual, or payment for the provision of health care to the individual.[6] HIPAA thus covers a wide range of health information, including but not limited to information about communicable disease. The state communicable disease confidentiality law applies *only* to information or records that identify a person who has or may have a communicable disease or condition that the state Commission for Public Health has made reportable. It doesn't apply to other types of health information, but it is nevertheless a law with a wide reach, as there are more than 70 reportable communicable diseases and conditions in North Carolina.

Third, the two laws have different rules regarding when information about communicable disease may be disclosed. In general, the state communicable disease confidentiality law is stricter than HIPAA about whether and to whom information may be disclosed. However, HIPAA is sometimes more prescriptive than the state law about the conditions that must be met before a disclosure is made. It is therefore important to consider HIPAA and state law together when deciding whether and how communicable disease information may be disclosed.

Overview of Relevant Provisions of the HIPAA Privacy Rule

The general rule under HIPAA is that an individual's written authorization is required before PHI may be disclosed.[7] However, there are several exceptions that expressly allow disclosure of PHI without the individual's

---

entity concept and its applicability to local government agencies in North Carolina, see Aimee Wall, *Should a Local Government Be a HIPAA Hybrid Entity?* COATES' CANONS LOCAL GOV'T L. BLOG (Apr. 28, 2015), http://canons.sog.unc.edu/should-a-local-government-be-a-hipaa-hybrid-entity/. The specific HIPAA rules that address hybrid entities are 45 C.F.R. §§ 164.103 (defining "hybrid entity" and related terms) & 164.105 (describing hybrid entity designation and the applicability of the HIPAA regulations to a hybrid entity).

6. 45 C.F.R. § 160.103.

7. 45 C.F.R. § 164.508(a).

authorization. Two of these exceptions, in particular, are relevant to communicable disease control and are discussed below.

Disclosures Required by Law

A HIPAA-covered entity may disclose PHI when the disclosure is required by law, so long as the disclosure complies with and is limited to the law's requirements.[8] The term "required by law" is defined to include statutes or regulations that require the production of information. In North Carolina, there are several state laws that require the disclosure of information to public health officials for communicable disease control purposes.

Disclosures for Public Health Purposes

A HIPAA-covered entity may disclose PHI to public health officials or agencies that are authorized by law to receive the information for various public health purposes, including preventing or controlling disease.[9] This HIPAA provision expressly extends to disease reporting, public health surveillance, public health investigations, and public health interventions.

The provision also expressly allows public health officials in HIPAA-covered entities to disclose information to persons who may be at risk of contracting a disease, but *only if* public health officials are authorized by law to make that disclosure. In North Carolina, that disclosure is authorized only if it satisfies the state communicable disease confidentiality law's requirement that the disclosure (1) be necessary to protect the public health and (2) be made in accordance with the state communicable disease control rules.

Overview of the State Communicable Disease Confidentiality Law

The state communicable disease confidentiality law has a general rule that is similar to HIPAA's—ordinarily, written consent is required to disclose information covered by the law.[10] Like HIPAA, the state communicable disease confidentiality law contains a number of exceptions to the general rule that written consent is required. Information that is subject to the

---

8. 45 C.F.R. § 164.512(a).

9. 45 C.F.R. § 164.512(b).

10. G.S. 130A-143. Written consent may be provided by the person identified in the record or by the person's legal guardian.

state law may be disclosed without written consent under the following circumstances:

- When disclosure is necessary to protect the public health and is made in accordance with the communicable disease control measure rules adopted by the Commission for Public Health.
- When disclosure is made pursuant to other provisions of G.S. Chapter 130A, Article 6 (the state statutes that set out the legal framework for communicable disease reporting, investigation, and control).
- When disclosure is made by a public health official to a court or a law enforcement official for purposes of enforcing the state communicable disease or public health bioterrorism laws.[11] A law enforcement official who receives the information is prohibited from disclosing it further except (1) when necessary to enforce the communicable disease or public health bioterrorism laws; (2) when necessary to investigate a terrorist incident involving a nuclear, biological, or chemical agent; or (3) when a public health official seeks the law enforcement official's assistance in preventing or controlling the spread of disease *and* expressly authorizes the law enforcement official to make disclosures as necessary to that purpose.
- When disclosure is made by a public health official to another federal, state, or local public health agency for the purpose of preventing or controlling the spread of a communicable disease or condition.
- When disclosure is made pursuant to a subpoena or court order, provided that upon the request of the person who is identified in the record, the record is reviewed in camera.[12]

---

11. The public health bioterrorism laws are found in G.S. Chapter 130A, Article 22. For an overview of those laws, see Jill Moore, *New North Carolina Public Health Bioterrorism Law*, HEALTH L. BULL. No. 79 (Feb. 2003), www.sog.unc.edu/publications/bulletins/new-north-carolina-public-health-bioterrorism-law.

12. HIPAA and North Carolina privilege laws also affect the disclosure of information pursuant to subpoenas or court orders. For more information, see John Rubin and Aimee Wall, *Responding to Subpoenas for Health Department Records*, HEALTH L. BULL. No. 82 (Sept. 2005), http://sogpubs.unc.edu/electronicversions/pdfs/hlb82.pdf.

- For purposes of "treatment," "payment," or "health care operations," as those terms are defined by HIPAA, and subject to the same conditions on those disclosures that HIPAA imposes.[13]
- For purposes of research, subject to limitations in HIPAA and state law.[14]

The state statute reflects the overarching importance of confidentiality to public health's communicable disease control system. Communicable disease information can be highly sensitive. There are many examples in history of communicable disease carrying stigma or resulting in adverse consequences for individuals. Because of this, people who suspect they have a communicable disease may be reluctant to seek diagnosis or treatment if they fear the information will become public. Maintaining confidentiality can therefore be seen as a communicable disease control measure in itself, because it promotes the detection of communicable disease—an essential step in controlling its spread. Indeed, in 1997, the North Carolina Supreme Court made clear that the state's confidentiality law was a critical element of the overall communicable disease control program: the Court upheld a state rule requiring the reporting of the names of individuals with HIV only *after* concluding that the state confidentiality law was sufficient to guard against unauthorized public disclosure of the information.[15]

---

13. *See* 45 C.F.R. § 164.506 (uses and disclosures for purposes of treatment, payment, and health care operations). For more information about how HIPAA defines and provides for disclosures for treatment, payment, and health care operations, see U.S. Department of Health and Human Services, *Uses and Disclosures for Treatment, Payment, and Health Care Operations*, www.hhs.gov/hipaa/for-professionals/privacy/guidance/disclosures-treatment-payment-health-care-operations/index.html.

14. There are two provisions in the state communicable disease law that address research. One allows any entity with information protected by the law to disclose the information for purposes of research as that term is defined by HIPAA and subject to the same conditions on research disclosures that HIPAA imposes. *See* 45 C.F.R. § 164.512(i) (uses and disclosures for research purposes). The other allows the state Department of Health and Human Services to disclose information for bona fide research purposes in accordance with laws adopted by the Commission for Public Health. *See* 10A N.C.A.C. 41A .0104.

15. Act-Up Triangle v. COMM'N FOR HEALTH SERVS., 345 N.C. 699, 712 (1997) ("We conclude that the statutory security provisions are adequate to protect against potential unlawful disclosure which might otherwise render the confidential HIV testing program constitutionally infirm").

Disclosure of Information That Is Not Identifiable

Both HIPAA and the state communicable disease confidentiality law allow disclosure of information that is not individually identifiable. The state law expressly authorizes release of "specific medical or epidemiological information for statistical purposes in a way that no person can be identified."[16] The HIPAA Privacy Rule allows disclosure of de-identified information and sets out very specific criteria that must be applied to determine whether information may be considered de-identified. In general, those criteria require one of two things: either a person who has been trained in statistical methodology must apply the appropriate methods and determine that the information has been de-identified, or particular identifiers must be stripped from the information. Before concluding that information has been de-identified and may be released, it is imperative to consult the relevant HIPAA provision to ensure that information has been de-identified properly.[17]

Obtaining Communicable Disease Information for Public Health Purposes

Obtaining Information through Communicable Disease Reports

Several statutes and rules require physicians and specified others to report known or suspected communicable diseases to public health officials.[18] Medical facilities are permitted, but not required, to make reports as well.[19] A person who makes a report is immune from any civil or criminal liability that might otherwise arise under state law.[20] A HIPAA-covered entity that makes a report need not worry about violating HIPAA, either, as the HIPAA Privacy Rule expressly allows these disclosures. Most communicable disease reports are required by state statutes and rules, so they fit under the HIPAA provision that authorizes disclosures that are required by law. Reports by medical facilities are *permitted* but not *required*, so they

---

16. G.S. 130A-143(1).

17. 45 C.F.R. § 164.514(a).

18. G.S. 130A-135 through -141.1; 10A N.C.A.C. 41A .0101 through .0106. For more information, see "Communicable Disease Reporting" in Chapter 2.

19. G.S. 130A-157.

20. G.S. 130A-142.

do not fit under the required-by-law provision. However, they do fit under the HIPAA provision that permits disclosures to public health officials who are authorized by law to receive the information for public health purposes, including disease reporting.[21]

Obtaining Information Relevant to a Case or an Outbreak Investigation

A North Carolina statute requires health care providers and others to allow public health officials to examine and copy records in their possession, including medical records, if the state health director or a local health director determines that the records pertain to

- the diagnosis, treatment, or prevention of a communicable disease or condition for a person who is infected, exposed, or reasonably suspected of having been infected or exposed; or
- the investigation of a known or reasonably suspected outbreak of a communicable disease or communicable condition.[22]

A public health official who seeks to examine or copy records under this provision must present proper identification and should also be prepared to show and explain the law that permits him or her to have access.[23] A health care provider who permits access to records pursuant to this statute is immune from any civil or criminal liability that might otherwise be imposed under state law.[24] The provider need not fear that he or she is violating HIPAA, either, since the HIPAA Privacy Rule expressly allows disclosures that are required by law.[25]

---

21. 45 C.F.R. § 164.512(b). HIPAA-covered entities should note that disclosures made pursuant to this section are subject to HIPAA's minimum necessary standard. 45 C.F.R. § 164.502(b); 164.514(d). Disclosures that are required by law *are not* subject to the minimum necessary standard. For more information about the minimum necessary standard, see U.S. Department of Health and Human Services, *Minimum Necessary Requirement*, www.hhs.gov/hipaa/for-professionals/privacy/guidance/minimum-necessary-requirement/index.html.

22. G.S. 130A-144(b).

23. *Id.*; see also 45 C.F.R. § 164.514(h), the HIPAA provision that requires covered entities to verify the identity and authority of a person requesting PHI.

24. G.S. 130A-144(c).

25. 45 C.F.R. § 164.512(a). Arguably, this statute also fits under the provision authorizing disclosures to public health officials who are authorized by law to receive the information for public health purposes, including disease investigation and control. 45 C.F.R. § 164.512(b). However, disclosures that fit into the second

Public Health Officials' Obligation to Maintain the Confidentiality of Communicable Disease Information

Public health officials who obtain communicable disease information for public health purposes must maintain the confidentiality of the information in accordance with the state communicable disease confidentiality law and any other laws that may apply to it, including HIPAA.

HIPAA and Communicable Disease Information Held by Public Health Agencies

If a public health entity that has communicable disease information is a HIPAA-covered entity (or a HIPAA-covered component of a hybrid entity), then the HIPAA Privacy Rule applies to information that it acquires, maintains, uses, or discloses for public health purposes. This does not mean that the information may not be used or disclosed; it just means that the information may be used or disclosed only as permitted by the HIPAA Privacy Rule.

Every local public health agency in North Carolina is subject to the HIPAA Privacy Rule. Some local agencies have completed a hybrid entity designation for either their department or their county, meaning that they have determined that some of their programs or activities are not required to comply with the HIPAA Privacy Rule. If a local agency has determined that some or all of its communicable disease activities are not part of the HIPAA-covered component, then HIPAA may not apply to *those particular activities* in *that particular locality*. Decisions about this are made locally, so it is not possible to make an across-the-board statement about the applicability of HIPAA to communicable disease activities in *every* local public health agency in North Carolina. Each local agency should have this information on file and should clearly communicate to its staff members which functions or activities are covered components. Information acquired,

---

category are subject to HIPAA's minimum necessary standard, while disclosures that are required by law are not. 45 C.F.R. § 164.502(b)(2)(v). The application of the minimum necessary standard could frustrate the purpose of the statute requiring the disclosure, as well as create significant administrative burdens for both the disclosing entity and the receiving public health official. *See* 45 C.F.R. § 164.514(d). It therefore seems unwise to place this in a category that would require application of the standard.

maintained, used, or disclosed by HIPAA-covered components is subject to the HIPAA Privacy Rule.

State Communicable Disease Confidentiality Law and Public Health Activities

The state communicable disease confidentiality law applies to all public health agencies, activities, and employees, regardless of whether HIPAA also applies. As the overview of the law earlier in this section makes clear, public health officials are authorized to disclose communicable disease information in a number of circumstances in order to carry out public health purposes. However, it is important to keep in mind that the law does not authorize unrestrained disclosure; any given disclosure needs to fit one or more of the particular circumstances specified in the statute.

The state law also specifies that any records that identify an individual who has or may have a reportable communicable disease are "strictly confidential" and not public records for purposes of G.S. Chapter 132 (the state law that gives the public access to most government records). This means that when a public agency has information that is subject to the state communicable disease confidentiality law in its records, the agency may not disclose that information in response to a public records request, even if the record is otherwise a public record that the public has a right to access.[26] However, sometimes the record in which the information is contained may

---

26. This is particularly significant because, if the record *were* subject to public access under G.S. Chapter 132, then HIPAA alone would not prohibit the disclosure of the information. The general rule for public agency records in North Carolina is that they must be made available to the public unless a specific statute excepts them from public access. The HIPAA Privacy Rule treats this as a "required by law" disclosure that is permitted under 45 C.F.R. § 164.512(a). *See* www.hhs.gov/ocr/privacy/hipaa/faq/disclosures_for_law_enforcement_purposes/506.html. Absent this protection in state law, the public records law would appear to compel the disclosure and HIPAA would not prevent it. Several North Carolina public health and health care statutes contain provisions stating that different categories of patient medical and financial records are not public records for purposes of G.S. Chapter 132. *See, e.g.*, G.S. 130A-12 (records containing privileged or protected patient information maintained by local health departments or the state Department of Health and Human Services are confidential and not public records as defined in G.S. 132-1); 130A-45.8 (medical records and patient financial records compiled and maintained by a public health authority are not public records as defined by G.S. Ch. 132); 131E-97 (medical records and patient financial records compiled and

be disclosed after the communicable disease information is redacted. A public health agency should consult with its attorney to determine how to respond to a request for records that may be subject to this protection.

Disclosing Information about Communicable Disease to the Public

Public health officials sometimes need to disclose information about communicable disease to the public. They may need to disclose information about a case or an outbreak in order to protect the public health. Public health officials also routinely make information about diseases in the population available to health care providers and others, as part of their role in assessing the community's health and keeping the public informed.

Considering HIPAA and state law together, it is possible to identify three circumstances in which communicable disease information may be disclosed publicly, either to the general public or to a subset potentially affected by the disease. Information may be disclosed publicly

1. with the individual's written authorization,
2. when disclosure of the information is necessary to protect the public health and is made in accordance with the North Carolina communicable disease control rules, or
3. when the information that is released is for statistical purposes only and cannot be used to identify an individual.

These circumstances are discussed in more detail below.

Public Disclosure with the Individual's Written Authorization

Both HIPAA and the state communicable disease confidentiality law allow communicable disease information to be made public if the individual who is the subject of the information gives written permission. If the entity disclosing the information is covered by HIPAA, the written permission must be given on a HIPAA-compliant authorization form.[27]

---

maintained by public hospitals and other public health care facilities are not public records as defined by G.S. Ch. 132).

27. *See* 45 C.F.R. § 164.508.

When and why would an individual want to authorize this type of disclosure? Probably the most common circumstance involves an individual who agrees to discuss his or her communicable disease experience with the media or other public outlets. Sometimes an individual will want a public health official or doctor to make a statement as well. An individual certainly may discuss his or her own health with the media or any person. However, if he or she wants a public health official or health care provider to discuss the individual's particular case, then he or she should provide written authorization that clearly identifies to whom information may be disclosed and specifies any limits on the information that may be disclosed. A public health official or health care provider who is asked to make a disclosure in this circumstance is not required to do so and should consider carefully whether it is a good idea.

Public Disclosure When the Information Is Necessary to Protect the Public Health and the Disclosure Is Made in Accordance with the North Carolina Communicable Disease Control Rules

Public health officials sometimes determine that they need to disclose information about a communicable disease case or outbreak in order to protect the public health. HIPAA allows public health officials to disclose information to persons who may be at risk of contracting a disease, but *only if* the public health officials are authorized by law to do so. North Carolina's communicable disease confidentiality law provides that authority, but *only if* disclosure (1) is necessary to protect the public health and (2) is allowed by the applicable communicable disease rules. This may be best illustrated with a couple of examples:

A restaurant employee is diagnosed with hepatitis A, a disease that can be transmitted by food handlers. The local health department investigates and determines that it needs to issue a press release to ensure that members of the public who may have been exposed to hepatitis A receive appropriate medical evaluation or treatment.

A child who attends a summer day camp is diagnosed with pertussis (whooping cough). The local health department determines that parents of other children attending the camp need to be notified that their child may have been exposed and advised about any prophylactic measures that should be taken.

In both of these cases, the disclosures the health department wishes to make would be allowed, because (1) disclosure is necessary to protect the public health, and (2) the communicable disease control rules for the diseases in each example allow the particular disclosure to be made. Both of these points require case-by-case decision making. In making the decision, it is important to remember that the communicable disease control rules are disease-specific and should be read closely before making a disclosure under this exception.

When this kind of disclosure is made, public health officials do not identify by name the person who had the communicable disease. However, for purposes of both HIPAA and the state communicable disease confidentiality law, this is still considered a disclosure of identifiable information, because it is possible (maybe even likely) that some members of the public will be able to figure out who the infected individual is. Public health officials should take care to disclose only the information that is needed to protect the public health in the particular circumstances, bearing in mind that a disclosure of this type is subject to HIPAA's minimum necessary standard. The minimum necessary standard requires covered entities to limit the amount of protected health information that is disclosed to the minimum that is needed to accomplish the purpose of the disclosure.[28]

Public Disclosure When the Information That Is Released Is for Statistical Purposes Only and Cannot Be Used to Identify an Individual

Public health officials are responsible for keeping other government officials and the general public informed about health conditions in the community. This may include disclosing statistical information about communicable diseases. Both HIPAA and the state communicable disease confidentiality law allow disclosure of information that does not identify individuals. If the entity releasing the information is a HIPAA-covered entity, the information must be de-identified in accordance with HIPAA's de-identification standard.[29] In general, the standard requires one of two things: either a person

---

28. 45 C.F.R. § 164.502(b); 164.514(d)(1). For more information about the minimum necessary standard, see U.S. Department of Health and Human Services, *Minimum Necessary Requirement*, www.hhs.gov/hipaa/for-professionals/privacy/guidance/minimum-necessary-requirement/index.html.

29. 45 C.F.R. § 164.514(a).

who has been trained in statistical methodology must apply the appropriate methods and determine that the information has been de-identified, or particular identifiers must be stripped from the information.

Part 2

Special Topics in North Carolina Communicable Disease Law

Chapter 6

Isolation and Quarantine

Isolation and quarantine are legal tools the public health system uses to control the spread of communicable diseases and conditions. The use of these tools in North Carolina is not extraordinary. Isolation and quarantine are used on a regular basis to control the spread of endemic diseases such as tuberculosis, as well as to cope with more unusual outbreaks, such as the measles outbreak the state experienced in 2013[1] or the pertussis (whooping cough) outbreaks that occasionally affect North Carolina schools. On rare occasions, the isolation and quarantine authorities have been used to control a more unusual event, such as the SARS case the state experienced in 2003.[2] Public health officials need to be aware of their authority to isolate and quarantine, and they need to know how to exercise the authority within the limits of the law.

Definition of Isolation and Quarantine

The terms "isolation" and "quarantine" are often used in conjunction, and they do have common elements. Both are communicable disease control measures—that is, they are means of preventing or containing the spread of disease. In general, medical and public health professionals use the term isolation to refer to disease control measures applied to people who are infected with a disease. The term quarantine generally refers to control measures applied to people who appear well but may nevertheless pose a

---

1. Kristin Sullivan, Zack S. Moore, & Aaron T. Fleischauer, *Notes from the Field: Measles Outbreak Associated with a Traveler Returning from India—North Carolina, April-May 2013*, MORBIDITY AND MORTALITY WEEKLY REPORT, Sept. 13, 2013, www.cdc.gov/mmwr/preview/mmwrhtml/mm6236a6.htm.

2. N.C. Division of Public Health, *SARS in North Carolina in 2003*, http://epi.publichealth.nc.gov/cd/sars/SARSinNorthCarolina2003.pdf (on file with author).

risk of disease to others—usually because they have been exposed to an ill person.

North Carolina's legal definitions of isolation and quarantine include but go beyond these general definitions. In North Carolina, "isolation authority" is the authority to limit the freedom of movement or freedom of action of a person or animal that has (or is suspected of having) a communicable disease or condition.[3] The definition of quarantine authority has three parts. It most often refers to the authority to limit the freedom of movement or action of a person or animal that has been exposed (or is suspected of having been exposed) to a communicable disease or condition. However, it also means the authority to limit access by any person or animal to an area or facility that is contaminated with an infectious agent. Quarantine authority also may be used to limit the freedom of movement or action of unimmunized persons during an outbreak.[4] For example, in the event of a measles outbreak, quarantine authority could be used to require children who are exempt from the state's immunization requirements to stay home from school.[5]

Both the isolation and quarantine authorities permit the limitation of a person's *freedom of movement* or *freedom of action*. The definition of quarantine also authorizes limits on *freedom of access*. No law defines these terms, but several other laws make important distinctions between orders that limit freedom of action and orders that limit freedom of movement or

---

3. N.C. GEN. STAT. (hereinafter G.S.) § 130A-2(3a).

4. G.S. 130A-2(7a). The term "quarantine" is also used to describe the local health director's authority to declare an area "under quarantine against rabies" when there is a rabies outbreak extensive enough to endanger the lives of humans. G.S. 130A-194. This book does not address rabies quarantines. For information about rabies quarantines, see Aimee N. Wall, *An Overview of North Carolina's Rabies Control Laws*, LOCAL GOV'T L. BULL. No. 125 (Oct. 2011), http://sogpubs .unc.edu/electronicversions/pdfs/lglb125.pdf.

5. All children in North Carolina are required to be immunized against certain diseases, including measles. G.S. 130A-152. The complete list of required immunizations is in the North Carolina Administrative Code. N.C. ADMIN. CODE (hereinafter N.C.A.C.) tit. 10A, ch. 41A, § .0401. Children who have not received the immunizations may not attend public or private day care centers or schools. G.S. 130A-155. However, a child may be exempt from the requirements if an immunization is medically contraindicated, G.S. 130A-156, 10A N.C.A.C. 41A .0404, or if the child's parent has a bona fide religious objection to immunization, G.S. 130A-157, 10A N.C.A.C. 41A .0403.

access. For example, Section 130A-145 of the North Carolina General Statutes (hereinafter G.S.), the main isolation and quarantine statute, provides specific procedures for a person to obtain judicial review of an isolation or quarantine order—but only if it is an order limiting freedom of movement or access. It is therefore important to understand the ways in which the limitations differ:

- An order limiting *freedom of movement* essentially prohibits an individual from going somewhere. It may confine the person to a particular place, such as his or her home or a health care facility. Or it may prohibit the person from going to a particular place. For example, it may prevent a person from returning to school or work during the period of communicability.
- An order limiting *freedom of action* affects specific behaviors but not the ability to move freely in society. For example, a person who is required to refrain from sexual activity during the course of treatment for gonorrhea has had his or her freedom of action restricted.
- An order limiting *freedom of access* prohibits a person from obtaining access to a certain place. For example, a quarantine order could be issued to prohibit a person from entering an area where infected people are being treated during an outbreak.

The use of these terms in North Carolina's statutory definitions also means that, in this state, an isolation or quarantine order does not necessarily require a person to be physically separated from the public. Rather, it directs the individual to comply with communicable disease control measures, which vary by disease and which may constitute limitations on freedom of movement, action, or access. For example, the control measures for a person with rubella (German measles) require the person to be isolated for seven days after the onset of the rash.[6] In contrast, the control measures for a person with HIV do not require physical separation from society but instead affect the individual's behavior.[7] Among other things,

---

6. H. McLean et al., *Rubella*, Ch. 14 *in* MANUAL FOR THE SURVEILLANCE OF VACCINE-PREVENTABLE DISEASES (Apr. 1, 2014), www.cdc.gov/vaccines/pubs/surv-manual/chpt14-rubella.html.

7. North Carolina law specifically prohibits public health officials from requiring a person with HIV to remain at home or otherwise be physically separated from

a person with HIV must notify sexual partners of his HIV status and must refrain from donating blood or sharing needles.[8] However, an order directing a person to comply with control measures for either condition is called an "isolation order." Similarly, an order directing a person who has been exposed to a communicable disease but is not yet sick is called a "quarantine order," whether it requires the person's physical separation from the public or simply directs the person to take (or refrain from taking) specific actions.

Ordering Isolation or Quarantine
Authority to Order Isolation or Quarantine

North Carolina law permits either the state health director or a local health director to order isolation or quarantine.[9] This authority may be delegated to another public official or employee.[10] Isolation or quarantine orders are permitted only (1) when and for so long as the public health is endangered, (2) when all other reasonable means for correcting the problem have been exhausted, and (3) when no less restrictive alternative exists.[11]

There is no law in North Carolina that interprets the phrase "all other reasonable means." The plain words of the statute make clear that, if there are reasonable means of controlling the public health threat short of issuing an isolation or quarantine order, those means should be tried first. But what constitutes reasonable means? The word "reasonable" could be interpreted to mean at least a couple of different things. It almost certainly should be

the general public. 10A N.C.A.C. 41A.0201(d) provides that isolation or quarantine orders for HIV may be no more restrictive than the control measures established in the North Carolina Administrative Code. The control measures for HIV do not include physical isolation. See 10A N.C.A.C. 41A .0202.

8. 10A N.C.A.C. 41A .0202.

9. G.S. 130A-145(a).

10. G.S. 130A-6. The statute states that a public official granted authority under G.S. Chapter 130A may delegate that authority to "another person authorized by the public official." Because isolation and quarantine are exercises of the state's police power, such a delegation should be made to another public official, not to a private person or entity. As part of their planning for responding to public health emergencies, local health directors in North Carolina have been strongly encouraged to designate health department staff members who are authorized to exercise the isolation or quarantine authority in the event the health director is unavailable.

11. G.S. 130A-145(a).

interpreted to mean that the only other methods that must be tried are those that are likely to be effective at controlling the public health threat. (In some cases there may be no other means believed to be effective.) It could also be interpreted to mean that public health officials need not try means that might be effective but that are unduly expensive or burdensome compared to isolation or quarantine.

Similarly, there is no law in North Carolina that interprets the phrase "less restrictive alternative." Assuming other reasonable means have been exhausted, when is isolation or quarantine the least restrictive alternative? There is no case law on this in North Carolina. Some other jurisdictions have addressed a similar issue—the involuntary civil confinement of individuals with tuberculosis—and have reached conclusions about when involuntary confinement of individuals with communicable disease is appropriate. Among other things, they have concluded the following:

- Involuntary confinement is not justified unless the person poses an actual danger to others. Even then, it should not be ordered if there is something else that could protect the public as effectively (such as directly observed therapy).[12]
- A person may be confined when he or she demonstrates unwillingness or inability to comply with less restrictive measures.[13]

Many public health scholars have viewed the confinement cases as instructive for isolation and quarantine cases.[14] However, in September 2016, a federal district court suggested that quarantine may require a different

---

12. *See, e.g.,* City of Newark v. J.S., 652 A.2d 265, 271, 278–79 (N.J. 1993). "Directly observed therapy" is defined in North Carolina law as "the actual observation of medication ingestion by a health care worker." 10A N.C.A.C. 41A .0205(g).

13. *See, e.g.,* City of New York City v. Doe, 614 N.Y.S.2d 8 (App. Div. 1994) (confinement in hospital for treatment of tuberculosis upheld when the evidence showed that the patient had a history of refusing to cooperate with directly observed therapy).

14. *See, e.g.,* LAWRENCE O. GOSTIN, PUBLIC HEALTH LAW: POWER, DUTY, RESTRAINT 444 (2d ed.) ("Although modern cases often concern civil commitment of the mentally ill, they should also apply to isolation and quarantine."); Wendy Parmet, *Ebola Quarantines: Remembering Less Restrictive Alternatives*, HARVARD L. BILL OF HEALTH BLOG (Oct. 26, 2014) (noting the scant case law on quarantine and relying on tuberculosis civil confinement cases to conclude that detention is permissible "only upon a showing that the patient has been non-compliant with less restrictive approaches").

type of analysis. In *Hickox v. Christie*,[15] the plaintiff was a nurse who had treated Ebola patients in Sierra Leone during the epidemic of 2014–2016. When she returned to the United States, she was quarantined and confined in an isolation tent outside a hospital while her health was monitored. The nurse subsequently brought an action under 42 U.S.C. § 1983, arguing that her constitutional rights were violated by the state officials who confined her. To make her case, the plaintiff needed to demonstrate that the state officials violated clearly established law. The court first reviewed prior cases specifically addressing quarantine, and it concluded that this body of law clearly establishes that quarantine is *not* unconstitutional—on the contrary, it is a valid exercise of the state's police power, so long as it is not unreasonable or arbitrary.[16] The court then considered the plaintiff's argument that civil commitment case law put the defendants on notice that their conduct violated clearly established law. It described the analogy to civil commitment law as "highly problematic,"[17] and its misgivings probably foreshadowed its ultimate conclusion that the civil commitment law did not create a clearly established constitutional right that the defendants violated.[18] Nevertheless, it considered the plaintiff's arguments, including the assertion that quarantine should not be used unless it is the least restrictive means available to protect the public health. The court concluded that "[t]he theoretical availability of less restrictive alternatives does not mean that they are appropriate for a particular individual" and that deference to public health officials was appropriate.[19]

If a North Carolina court were called upon to determine when isolation or quarantine is the least restrictive alternative, it is likely that the court would consider other courts' conclusions about what that means. At present, however, those other courts' conclusions offer different paths,

---

15. ___ F. Supp. 3d ___, No. 15-7647, 2016 WL 4744181 (D.N.J. Sept. 2, 2016).

16. *Id.* at *10. The court appeared open to a different conclusion if different facts suggested that quarantine was not warranted, but found that the facts of this case "do not suggest arbitrariness or unreasonableness as recognized in the prior cases—i.e., application of the quarantine laws to a person (or, more commonly, vast numbers of persons) who had no exposure to disease at all." *Id.*

17. *Id.* at *10.

18. *Id.* at *18.

19. *Id.* at *15 (concluding that the determination is a judgment call, and that the decision to confine the plaintiff in this case was one a reasonable public health official could have reached, even if it "could be criticized, or portrayed as erroneous").

with the recent federal court decision in the Ebola quarantine case being significantly more deferential to public health officials' judgments.

Decision to Order Isolation or Quarantine

Individuals in North Carolina are legally obliged to comply with communicable disease control measures regardless of whether an isolation or quarantine order has been issued to them.[20] Failure to comply is a misdemeanor.[21] Still, health directors often issue isolation or quarantine orders to ensure that a person who is subject to communicable disease control measures is aware of the measures and of the legal obligation to comply. It is also common for a health director to issue an isolation or quarantine order to an individual who is not complying with control measures, as part of an effort to gain compliance.

The authority to order isolation or quarantine is not limited to reportable diseases or conditions. However, for the isolation or quarantine authority to be available, the illness must satisfy the statutory definition of "communicable disease" or "communicable condition."

How Isolation or Quarantine Is Ordered

There is no North Carolina statute or rule that sets forth specific steps to follow in ordering isolation or quarantine of a person. However, by considering all the various laws together, it is possible to reach a few conclusions about how to proceed:

1. A local health director or the state health director should ensure that he or she is authorized to exercise isolation or quarantine authority in the particular situation, as follows:

   - If the person is to be isolated, he or she must be infected or reasonably suspected of being infected with a communicable disease or condition.
   - If the person is to be quarantined, he or she must meet the statutory conditions for quarantine, which usually means that he or she has been exposed or is reasonably suspected

---

20. G.S. 130A-144(f).
21. G.S. 130A-25.

of having been exposed to a communicable disease or condition.[22]

- The public health must be endangered as a result.
- All other reasonable means for controlling the disease must have been exhausted.
- There must be no less restrictive means to protect the public health.

2. The local or state health director must determine which of the following communicable disease control measures the recipient of the order will be subject to:

- Control measures for HIV, hepatitis B, sexually transmitted diseases, tuberculosis, smallpox/vaccinia disease, SARS, and hepatitis C, published in the North Carolina Administrative Code.[23]
- Control measures for other diseases, derived from recommendations and guidelines issued by the Centers for Disease Control and Prevention (CDC). If there are no CDC guidelines on point, control measures are derived from the American Public Health Association's *Control of Communicable Diseases Manual.* A public health official may also devise control measures if necessary, in accordance with principles set out in a state rule.[24]

3. The local or state health director must communicate to the person that he or she is being placed under an isolation or quarantine order. Although the law does not state that an isolation or quarantine order must be in writing, it would be unwise to rely solely on an oral order. However, it may be reasonable in some

---

22. This applies to the most typical situation in which isolation or quarantine is ordered, but quarantine may also be ordered for two additional reasons: to limit access to an area or facility that may be contaminated by an infectious agent or to limit the freedom of movement of unimmunized persons in an outbreak. *See* G.S. 130A-2(7a).

23. 10A N.C.A.C. 41A .0202 (HIV), .0203 (hepatitis B), .0204 (sexually transmitted diseases), .0205 (tuberculosis), .0208 (smallpox and vaccinia disease), .0213 (SARS), .0214 (hepatitis C).

24. 10 N.C.A.C. 41A .0201(a).

circumstances to issue an oral order and then follow it with a written order as soon as practicable.

4. An isolation or quarantine order should include the following:

- The name of the person who is subject to the order
- The names of the health department and the health director issuing the order
- A statement of the required communicable disease control measures
- A statement that the control measures have been explained to the person
- If the order limits the person's freedom of movement or freedom of access, a statement that the person has a right to have a court review the order
- A statement describing the penalties that may be imposed if the person fails to comply with the order[25]
- The signature of the health director or official with delegated authority who issued the order
- The date and time the order was issued

The North Carolina Division of Public Health often provides template isolation and quarantine orders during an outbreak. For example, during the SARS outbreak of 2003, the division sent template orders to all local health directors by email. Template orders that may be used in the event of a flu pandemic have been developed and are available on the Internet.[26]

Duration of Isolation or Quarantine Orders
Public Health Official's Order
The basic limitation on the duration of an isolation or quarantine order is contained in G.S. 130A-145(a), which states that isolation and quarantine may be ordered only when *and for so long as* the public health is endangered. The period of time is therefore likely to vary depending upon the communicable disease or condition and possibly other circumstances.

---

25. 10A N.C.A.C. 41A .0201(d).

26. The documents are part of the North Carolina Pandemic Influenza Plan. The plan is available at http://epi.publichealth.nc.gov/cd/flu/plan.html. The template orders are in Appendix L.

There is no maximum time limit for orders limiting *freedom of action*, other than the statute's requirement that the orders end when the public health is no longer endangered. For example, an order directing a person with HIV to refrain from donating blood could be in place for years,[27] while an order directing a person with a suspected low-risk exposure to the Ebola virus to participate in symptom monitoring would last only for the incubation period of the virus (presently recognized to be 21 days following the last exposure).[28]

Orders limiting *freedom of movement* or *freedom of access* are subject to a statutory maximum period of 30 days.[29] This is *in addition to* the requirement that the order last only for so long as the public health is endangered. As previously noted, an order limiting freedom of movement or access might be for less than 30 days—if, for example, it was a quarantine order issued to a person exposed to a disease with an incubation period of 21 days—but it may never exceed 30 days, even if the person is still a threat to the public health at the end of that period. As discussed below, however, a health director may petition a superior court to extend an order.

Petitions to Extend an Order beyond 30 Days

In some instances, the state health director or a local health director may determine that a person's freedom of movement must be restricted for more than 30 days in order to protect the public health. However, the health director does not have the authority to extend the initial order or to issue a second order to the same individual for the same communicable disease event. Instead, the director may petition a superior court to extend the order. Ordinarily, this action is instituted in the superior court in the county in which the limitation on freedom of movement was imposed. However, if the individual who is the subject of the order has already sought review of the order in Wake County superior court (see the next section on due process rights), then the action must be instituted in Wake County.[30]

The health director has the burden of producing sufficient evidence to support the extension. If the court determines by a preponderance of the evidence that the limitation on freedom of movement is reasonably neces-

---

27. 10A N.C.A.C. 41A .0202(a)(3) establishes this control measure.
28. *See* www.apha.org/~/media/files/pdf/pubs/ccdm_ebola.ashx.
29. G.S. 130A-145(d).
30. *Id.*

sary to prevent or limit the spread of the disease or condition, the court shall continue the limitation for a period of up to 30 days for any communicable disease or condition but tuberculosis. For tuberculosis, the court may extend the order for up to one year.

When necessary, the health director may return to court and ask the court to continue a limitation for additional periods of up to 30 days each (or up to one year each if the person has tuberculosis).

Due Process Rights of Isolated or Quarantined Persons

North Carolina law explains specifically how a person who is substantially affected by a limitation on freedom of movement or access may obtain a review of the order.[31] The person may institute an action in superior court seeking review of the limitation, and the court must respond by conducting a hearing within 72 hours (excluding Saturdays and Sundays). The person is entitled to an attorney. If he or she is indigent, a court-appointed attorney must be provided.

The court must terminate or reduce the limitation if it determines by a preponderance of the evidence that the limitation is not reasonably necessary to prevent or limit the spread of the disease or condition. The burden of producing sufficient evidence to show that the limitation is not reasonably necessary is on the person affected by the order. The person has a choice of where to file this action: either in the superior court of the county where the limitation is imposed or in the Wake County superior court.

A person who is subject to a limitation on freedom of action has a right to due process, which includes the opportunity for his or her objections to the order to be heard. However, North Carolina law does not spell out how a person subject to this kind of limitation may exercise this right. Most likely, the person would file an action in superior court seeking a declaratory judgment about the validity of the order, or the person would seek an injunction barring enforcement of the order.

---

31. *Id.* The statute does not define the term *substantially affected person*. It seems clear that the person who is the subject of the order would be a substantially affected person, but whether the term might include others is an open question.

Chapter 7

Bloodborne Pathogen Exposures

Some communicable diseases or conditions are caused by bloodborne pathogens. A *pathogen* is an agent that can cause disease, such as a virus or bacterium. A pathogen is considered *bloodborne* if it is present in human blood. When one person comes into contact with another person's blood or body fluids, there is the possibility of being exposed to a bloodborne pathogen. Because of this risk, federal and state communicable disease laws address bloodborne pathogen exposures. The laws define what constitutes an exposure and specify the follow-up measures that must occur to prevent or mitigate the risk that an infection will be transmitted. Three bloodborne pathogens that are of particular public health significance are addressed by these laws: human immunodeficiency virus (HIV), hepatitis B virus (HBV), and hepatitis C virus (HCV).[1]

There are a number of different ways a bloodborne pathogen exposure might occur, so the laws apply to a wide range of scenarios. The following are just a few examples:

- A health care worker is accidentally stuck by a needle that has been used on a patient
- A law enforcement officer is bitten by a person the officer is attempting to arrest
- A child finds a used syringe in a public park and pricks her finger on the needle

---

1. While these are not the only diseases that can be transmitted through human blood, they are targeted by the bloodborne pathogen laws because they pose the greatest risk of bloodborne disease transmission in occupational settings. *See* Occupational Safety and Health Administration, Final Rule: Occupational Exposure to Bloodborne Pathogens; Needlestick and Other Sharps Injuries, 66 Fed. Reg. 5318, 5318 (Jan. 18, 2001) (identifying HIV, HBV, and HCV as the "primary agents of concern in current occupational settings").

- A passerby assisting a person who has been injured is exposed to the injured person's blood

Two Sources of Regulation: OSHA Standards and North Carolina Rules

Which regulations apply to bloodborne pathogen exposures depends on whether an exposure occurs as part of a person's employment. Exposures experienced by an employee who is on the job are occupational exposures. Exposures that are unrelated to the activities of employment may be called either non-occupational or community exposures. When there is an occupational exposure, federal occupational safety and health rules (the OSHA standards) may apply. When an exposure occurs in the community or involves a person who isn't covered by the occupational safety and health rules, North Carolina's communicable disease control rules apply.

The Universal Precautions Approach

Both the OSHA standards and the North Carolina communicable disease rules take a "universal precautions" approach to bloodborne pathogen exposures. Universal precautions are the methods that are used to avoid exposure to pathogens when contact with blood or body fluids is anticipated. For example, the gloves and other personal protective equipment used by health care workers when dealing with patients, lab samples, or medical waste are universal precautions.

The precautions are called "universal" because they are used any time there might be contact with blood or certain body fluids, without regard to whether the particular person is known or suspected of having a bloodborne pathogen.[2] This approach reflects the reality that it is not always possible to know whether any given person is infected with a bloodborne pathogen. Even the infected individuals themselves may not know,[3] or they may not be able or willing to communicate the information at the

---

2. The federal Occupational Safety and Health Administration (OSHA) defines "universal precautions" as "an approach to infection control" in which "all human blood and certain human body fluids are treated as if known to be infectious." 29 C.F.R. § 1910.1030(b).

3. See, e.g., Centers for Disease Control and Prevention, *HIV in the United States: At a Glance* (Dec. 2, 2016), www.cdc.gov/hiv/statistics/overview/ataglance.html.

time of exposure. And there are some cases, such as exposures to needles that are improperly discarded, in which the exposed person wouldn't know whose infectious status to inquire about. By assuming that *any* individual *might* be infected, the universal precautions approach allows individuals who know they are at risk of exposure to blood or body fluids to protect themselves without having to inquire about or investigate each person's infectious status.

Other Similarities and Differences

The OSHA standards and the state communicable disease rules are similar in several important ways:

- They define exposure similarly.
- Both sets of rules require post-exposure evaluation and follow-up. Key components of the follow-up include testing the source person for HIV, HBV, and HCV and offering post-exposure testing, information, and sometimes treatment to the exposed person.
- The rules address only *non-sexual* exposures. They are designed for situations in which a worker or other person has an unintentional contact with blood or body fluids that occurred in the absence of (or despite the use of) universal precautions. There are other communicable disease control measures designed to protect individuals from acquiring a bloodborne pathogen through sexual contact.[4]
- Both sets of rules are a type of universal precaution applied without regard to whether a source person is suspected of being infected.

A key difference between the two sets of rules is the determination of who is responsible for doing what. In an occupational exposure, the workplace should have policies and procedures for following up with the employees involved. In community exposures, follow-up duties fall on the attending physicians of the exposed person and the source person. In practice, in community exposures local health departments often step into the role assigned to one or both of the attending physicians, either because one or

---

4. For example, North Carolina's HIV control measures require infected individuals to notify their sexual partners that they have HIV and to use condoms during sexual intercourse. N.C. ADMIN. CODE (hereinafter N.C.A.C.) tit. 10A, ch. 41A, § .0202.

both parties lack a physician, or because a party's physician is unfamiliar with the community exposure rules and seeks the department's assistance.

Occupational Exposures

The federal Occupational Safety and Health Administration (OSHA) adopted the OSHA bloodborne pathogen standards,[5] which apply to all occupational exposures to blood or "other potentially infectious materials" (OPIM) as defined in the standard.[6]

In addition to addressing bloodborne pathogen exposure incidents, the OSHA standards require employers to have, and to annually update, a written exposure control plan. The plan must identify workers who may have an exposure and address how occupational exposures may be eliminated or minimized. The standards also require employees to implement universal precautions in which all human blood and OPIM are treated as if they were known to be infectious. Employers must also provide appropriate personal protective equipment to workers and make hepatitis B vaccination available to all workers who may have an occupational exposure.

The OSHA standards define an exposure incident as "a specific eye, mouth, other mucous membrane, non-intact skin, or parenteral contact with blood or other potentially infectious materials that results from the performance of an employee's duties."[7] When an incident occurs, evaluation and follow-up must be provided at no cost to the employee.

The follow-up must include identifying the source person—that is, the person whose blood or OPIM was involved in the exposure[8]—and testing the source person for HIV and HBV.[9] The standards also require employers

---

5. 29 C.F.R., pt. 1910, subpart Z. The OSHA standards are incorporated by reference in North Carolina, at 13 N.C.A.C. 07A .0603, .0606.

6. "Other potentially infectious materials" includes any body fluid that is visibly contaminated with blood, as well as specified other body fluids. 29 C.F.R. § 1910.1030. The full definition is in the glossary in Appendix 1 of this book.

7. 29 C.F.R. § 1910.1030(b). *Parenteral contact* means an event that pierces the skin barrier, such as a needlestick or cut.

8. The OSHA standards refer to this person as the "source individual." The term "source person" is used here because that is the term used in the North Carolina communicable disease rules and the meaning is the same.

9. The OSHA standards specify that the source individual should be tested if he or she consents or if the law does not require consent. The North Carolina communicable disease rules require testing of source persons with or without their

to test the exposed person if he or she consents to testing and to offer post-exposure prophylaxis and counseling.

Non-occupational (Community) Exposures

Bloodborne pathogen exposures that are not addressed by the OSHA regulations are covered by North Carolina's communicable disease control rules. Three separate sections of the communicable disease rules address bloodborne pathogens: the rules establishing control measures for (1) HIV,[10] (2) hepatitis B,[11] and (3) hepatitis C.[12] These separate provisions are similar but not identical. In practice, they should be considered simultaneously to answer three questions:

1. Is the incident an exposure, as defined in the rules? If the answer is no, then the rules do not apply, and there is no need to proceed further.
2. Is the exposure of a type that would create a significant risk of transmission of a bloodborne pathogen? Again, if the answer is no, then the rules do not apply, and the inquiry ends here.
3. What are the specific follow-up steps that are required?

Exposure Incidents

A bloodborne pathogen exposure incident occurs when a person experiences either (1) a needlestick or (2) another type of non-sexual contact in which the blood or body fluids of one person (the source person) come into contact with the non-intact skin or mucous membrane of another person (the exposed person) *and* the contact is of a nature that would pose a significant risk of transmission of a bloodborne pathogen if the source person were infected.

A needlestick is always considered an exposure. For any other event to be considered an exposure, several criteria must be met. First, one person's blood or body fluids must make contact with another person's mucous membrane (such as the mouth or nasal passages) or non-intact skin (such

---

consent, but health care providers should proceed with caution when a source person refuses a test. See the discussion later in this chapter about how to manage this situation.

10. 10A N.C.A.C. 41A .0202(4).
11. 10A N.C.A.C. 41A .0203(b)(4).
12. 10A N.C.A.C. 41A .214(4).

as skin that has a cut or abrasion). Second, the contact must be non-sexual in nature. Third, the non-sexual contact must be of a type that *would* create a significant risk of transmission *if* the other person were infected. The conditional language of "would" and "if" is very important in these rules, because it reflects the rules' universal precaution approach: when there is an exposure, the rules do not apply only to individuals who are known or suspected of being infected with a pathogen. Instead, the rules assume the possibility that a bloodborne pathogen is present and require consideration of whether the exposure was of a type that would create a significant risk of transmission.

Significant Risk of Transmission

What constitutes a significant risk of transmission is determined on a case-by-case basis, taking into account current scientific knowledge on disease transmission risk. The determination should also consider the following factors, if information about these factors is available:

- The type of body fluid or tissue involved
- The volume of body fluid or tissue
- The concentration of the pathogen in the body fluid or tissue involved in the exposure
- The virulence of the pathogen in the body fluid or tissue
- The type of exposure (intact or non-intact skin or mucous membranes)[13]

Who makes the determination of whether an incident has created a significant risk of transmission? The rules do not directly address this question. However, they require the weighing of factors that must be understood in light of current scientific knowledge about bloodborne disease transmission. It is also worth noting that the rules put the duty of taking appropriate follow-up steps on the physicians of the parties involved in an exposure incident. This suggests that the determination of whether a given incident creates a significant risk of transmission should be made by a health care provider or public health professional who either has the relevant knowledge or is able to obtain and interpret information provided by others with

---

13. 10A N.C.A.C. 41A .0201(f). The concentration and virulence of the pathogen are probably the factors that are least likely to be known in a community exposure, as information from laboratory tests would be needed.

relevant expertise. The North Carolina Division of Public Health has communicable disease experts who are available to consult with health care providers or local health directors who must make this determination.[14]

Required Follow-Up

The state rules prescribe specific follow-up steps for an exposure incident. But before determining which follow-up steps to take, a physician or local health department must distinguish between the *source person(s)* and the *exposed person(s)* in the incident.

Source Person and Exposed Person

When an exposure incident occurs, there is at least one exposed person and at least one source person. An exposed person is a person whose non-intact skin or mucous membrane comes into contact with another person's blood or body fluids. A source person is a person whose blood or body fluids come into contact with another person's mucous membrane or non-intact skin.

These definitions seem straightforward, but they can produce counter-intuitive results. Compare the following two examples:

Bleeder has a bad nosebleed. Assistant, a bystander, offers help. In the course of assisting Bleeder, Assistant gets some of Bleeder's blood on her hands, where she has broken skin from a cut that is healing. Assistant is the exposed person. Bleeder is the source person.

Biter bites Victim, breaking his skin and drawing blood. Biter's mouth, a mucous membrane, is exposed to Victim's blood. This means that Biter is an *exposed* person and Victim is a *source* person. Sympathy for the victim can make this result feel counterintuitive—perhaps especially if Victim must submit to blood tests in the follow-up steps—but the focus of the bloodborne pathogen rules is on preventing disease transmission, without regard to who is at fault in creating the exposure incident.

Adding to the complexity, it is also possible for a person to be both a source person and an exposed person. The biting example illustrates this. It may be that the victim is an exposed person as well as a source person

---

14. The North Carolina Division of Public Health's Communicable Disease branch may be reached by telephone 24 hours a day at 919.733.3419.

because he or she has been exposed to the biter's saliva, a body fluid. But whether the victim is considered an exposed person would depend on a determination of whether exposure to saliva created a significant risk of transmission.[15] This is a question that should be answered by public health officials or health care providers who are familiar with both the current science about bloodborne pathogens and the factors they are required to consider in determining whether an exposure creates a significant risk of transmission.

The source person in an incident may be known or unknown. An example of an unknown source person is someone who finds an improperly disposed hypodermic needle and accidentally sticks herself with it. The procedures that the bloodborne pathogen rules prescribe to follow-up an exposure incident vary depending on whether the source person is known or unknown.

Required Follow-up: Source Person Unknown

When the source person is unknown, the follow-up steps that should be taken are all focused on the exposed person. The specific follow-up steps are found in three different state rules—the ones prescribing control measures for HIV, HBV, and HCV[16]—but they should be carried out concurrently rather than sequentially to the extent possible.

HIV. The attending physician of an exposed person with an unknown source person must give the exposed person information about the risk of HIV transmission and must offer HIV testing as soon as possible after exposure and then again at reasonable intervals for up to one year.[17] The communicable disease rules do not address any other follow-up steps, such as offering HIV prophylaxis, but of course health care providers should practice in accordance with the standard of care. If the standard of care

---

15. In many cases, exposure to saliva alone will not be considered to create a significant risk of transmission. The OSHA standards do not include saliva as an "other potentially infectious material" unless the exposure occurs in a dental procedure or the saliva is visibly contaminated by blood.

16. 10A N.C.A.C. 41A .0202(f), .0203(b)(4), and .0214(4), respectively.

17. If an HIV test is positive, both the physician and the exposed person must comply with additional HIV control measures contained in 10A N.C.A.C. 41A .0202. Laboratory-confirmed HIV must be reported to public health officials. G.S. 130A-135; 10A N.C.A.C. 41A .0101(29).

requires additional steps, they should take them or make appropriate referrals.

Hepatitis B Virus (HBV). The follow-up measures for HBV are set by CDC guidelines. They are a bit different than those for HIV or HCV, because there is an effective HBV vaccination.[18] Under the most recent CDC guidelines, further treatment is not required if the exposed person has completed the HBV vaccination series. In the absence of documentation of vaccination, however, the HBV vaccine series should be offered.[19] Note that CDC guidelines can and often do change as science develops, so current guidelines should be consulted.

Hepatitis C (HCV). When the source person is unknown, the exposed person's attending physician must advise the exposed person to seek testing for hepatitis C as soon as possible and again four to six months after the exposure.[20] The exposed person is not required to *be tested*—the requirement is that he or she *be advised to seek testing*. If the exposed person is tested and the test is positive, the attending physician must advise the person of the risk of transmitting the infection to others.[21]

Required Follow-up: Source Person Known

When the source person is known, the follow-up that is required is more complicated and involves both the source person and the exposed person. In general, there are three activities that must occur: notification, tests, and follow-up health care. The follow-up health care varies for each of the conditions (HIV, HBV, and HCV), but the notifications and testing requirements are substantially similar. Notification and testing may be considered a single step in the follow-up process, though there are multiple sub-steps.

Notification and testing. The exposed person's attending physician or health care provider must notify the source person's attending physician

---

18. HBV vaccination is required for children in North Carolina who were born on or after July 1, 1994. *See* G.S. 130A-153; 10A N.C.A.C. 41A .0401(7).

19. 10A N.C.A.C. 41A .0203(b)(4) incorporates the CDC guidelines by reference.

20. 10A N.C.A.C. 41A .0214(4)(b).

21. Acute hepatitis C is a reportable condition. G.S. 130A-135; 10A N.C.A.C. 41A .0101(28). A case definition of acute hepatitis C is available in the *North Carolina Communicable Disease Control Manual* at http://epi.publichealth.nc.gov/cd/lhds/manuals/cd/reportable_diseases.html.

that an exposure has occurred.[22] When the source person's physician receives the information, the physician must discuss the exposure with the source person and, unless the source person's infectious status is already known, must test the source person for HIV, HBV, and HCV.[23] The source person's physician must notify the exposed person's physician of the test results, and the exposed person's physician must then notify the exposed person. In other words, the exposed person will ultimately be told the results of the source person's tests. The physician must also instruct the exposed person that the information must be kept confidential.[24]

Follow-up health care. After the notification and testing process is completed, the exposed person's physician must provide specific follow-up care for each of the three pathogens of concern.

For HIV, the physician must offer the exposed person an HIV test as soon as possible after the exposure and then again at reasonable intervals for up to a year.[25] If it is determined that the source person was infected with HIV, the exposed person should be informed of the HIV control measures and should be offered or referred for other treatment in accordance with the standard of care.

For HBV, the follow-up depends on the exposed person's vaccination status. If the source is infected and the exposed person *has not* been vaccinated, the exposed person should be given hepatitis B immune globulin (HBIG) immediately and should begin the HBV vaccine series within seven days. If the source person is infected and the exposed person *has* been vaccinated, then the exposed person should be tested for the level of antibodies that are present in his or her blood. If the antibodies are below a certain level, the person should be offered HBIG and re-vaccination no later

---

22. To facilitate this process, health care facilities are expressly authorized to release the name of a source person's attending physician to the exposed person's physician. 10A N.C.A.C. 41A .0202(4)(c). If the source person does not have an attending physician, the local health department may carry out the duties of the source person's physician.

23. The testing requirement is found in three separate rules: 10A N.C.A.C. 41A .0202(4)(a)(1), .0203(b)(4)(A), .0214(4)(a).

24. *See* 10A N.C.A.C. 41A .0202(4); *see also* G.S. 130A-143 (individually identifiable communicable disease information and records are strictly confidential, regardless of whether the information is publicly or privately maintained, and may be released only as provided by law and the communicable disease rules).

25. 10A N.C.A.C. 41A .0202(4).

than seven days after exposure. (A level is specified in the communicable disease rules, but it is also wise to check with state communicable disease experts for recommendations regarding current standard of care and best practices.) The rules do not address what to do if the source is negative and the exposed person is unvaccinated, but because hepatitis B vaccine is now universally recommended, it would be wise to offer or refer the individual for the vaccine.[26]

For HCV, if the source person is infected, the exposed person's attending physician must advise the exposed person to seek HCV testing as soon as possible and again four to six months after exposure. The physician must also inform the exposed person of the hepatitis C control measures. Treatment for hepatitis C is rapidly evolving, so it is a good idea to consult with a communicable disease expert for the most up-to-date recommendations for the exposed person.

Refusal of Required Tests

The North Carolina communicable disease rules *require* tests for source persons. (Tests must be offered or encouraged for exposed persons, but they are not required.) What if a source person refuses a test that is required by the rules? The rules state that a source person may be tested with or without consent, so long as the test can be done with safety to the source person and the health care provider. In practice, providers should proceed with care if a source person refuses. There are several steps that may be taken if this occurs.

An attending physician may try to persuade a source person to have the test. However, the provider should not restrain the person and force the person to be tested. Instead, a source person who refuses testing should be reported to the local health director,[27] who has legal authority to obtain

---

26. Hepatitis B is a required vaccine for children in North Carolina, but the requirement applies only to those born on or after July 1, 1994. 10A N.C.A.C. 41A .0401.

27. Confidentiality laws expressly allow this disclosure of information. The HIPAA Privacy Rule authorizes disclosures to public health officials who are authorized by law to receive the information for disease control purposes. 45 C.F.R. § 164.512(b). North Carolina's communicable disease confidentiality law authorizes disclosures that are necessary to protect the public health and made as prescribed by the communicable disease rules. G.S. 130A-143(4). A state communicable

information from other sources and to enforce the communicable disease rules.

There are several actions a local health director may take. First, the director may be able to obtain information about the source person's HIV, hepatitis B, or hepatitis C status from existing records. The director has legal authority to get access to medical or laboratory records for this purpose.[28] Second, the director may order testing of an existing sample of the source person's blood if one happens to be available.[29] The person's blood usually is not available in the case of a community exposure, but this is worth keeping in mind. Third, the health director may order the source person to comply with the testing. State law requires all persons to comply with communicable disease control measures established by the Commission for Public Health, which includes the state bloodborne pathogen rules.[30] If the person declines to comply, the health director can use the legal remedies described in Chapter 4.

disease rule authorizes a physician to request that the local health director instruct a person to follow communicable disease control measures. 10A N.C.A.C. 41A .0210.

28. G.S. 130A-144(b).

29. 10A N.C.A.C. 41A .0202(4), .0214(4).

30. G.S. 130A-144(f).

Chapter 8

Bioterrorism and Public Health

In October 2001, shortly following the terrorist attacks of September 11 of that year, the United States was beset by an act of bioterrorism—the dissemination of anthrax through the mail. Twenty-three individuals contracted anthrax; five died.

The anthrax letter attacks spurred a new national focus on public health laws, particularly the state laws that prescribe the role, duties, and powers of public health systems. In North Carolina, a review of state public health laws revealed that some of the fundamental legal tools for responding to bioterrorism were in place. The state's communicable disease laws, in particular, provided some means for detecting and containing a threat caused by a biological agent. However, those laws were not designed to address terrorism specifically. In 2002, the North Carolina General Assembly enacted legislation with the short title, "Public Health Bioterrorism Preparedness."[1] Among other things, the legislation

- defined "public health threat" and authorized the state health director to order tests and investigations to determine whether a public health threat exists due to bioterrorism;
- gave public health officials access to otherwise confidential information about symptoms, syndromes, and trends that could indicate a public health threat caused by bioterrorism;
- created explicit legal protections for individuals who are affected by certain public health orders; and
- fostered planning and communication among state agencies that are likely to have a role in responding to a bioterrorist attack.

---

1. S.L. 2002-179 (H 1508), now codified as Chapter 130A, Article 22, of the North Carolina General Statutes (hereinafter G.S.).

Public Health Threats Caused by Terrorism

A "public health threat" is defined as "a situation that is likely to cause an immediate risk to human life, an immediate risk of serious physical injury or illness, or an immediate risk of serious adverse health effects."[2] North Carolina's public health bioterrorism laws authorize the state health director to exercise certain powers when he or she reasonably suspects two things: (1) that a public health threat may exist, and (2) that the threat may have been caused by a terrorist incident using nuclear, biological, or chemical agents.[3] The powers that the state health director may exercise in this circumstance can be divided into two categories: powers over property and powers over people and animals. They may be exercised only when and for so long as a public health threat may exist, all other reasonable means for correcting the problem have been exhausted, and no less restrictive alternative exists.

The state health director's powers to act on public health threats caused by terrorism are not shared with local health directors—they reside with the state health director alone. This is different from most of North Carolina's communicable disease laws, which permit either the state health director or a local health director to exercise authority that is statutorily granted. The powers are limited to the state level in large part because they are intended for exceptional cases that are not routinely encountered. Notably, the bioterrorism law expressly states that its provisions do not limit other legal authority granted to local or state public health officials in Chapter 130A of the North Carolina General Statutes.[4] For example, the law granting isolation and quarantine authority to both the state health director and local health directors is not limited or replaced by the state health director's bioterrorism-specific powers.

---

2. G.S. 130A-475(d).
3. G.S. 130A-475(a).
4. G.S. 130A-475(c).

State Health Director Powers over Property

When the state health director reasonably suspects that there may be a public health threat caused by bioterrorism, he or she may order tests to be performed on the property, close or evacuate property for the purpose of public health investigation, or order abatement of a public health threat.

Tests for Contamination

The state health director may test any real or personal property to determine the presence of nuclear, biological, or chemical agents.[5]

Closing or Evacuating Property for Evacuations

The state health director may evacuate or close any real property suspected of being contaminated by nuclear, biological, or chemical agents in order to investigate. The closure may not exceed 10 calendar days. If a longer period of time is required to complete the investigation, the director may ask a superior court to order that the property remain closed until the investigation is completed.[6]

Order to Abate a Public Health Threat

The state health director may order any action to abate a public health threat that may exist because of contamination of property as a result of bioterrorism.[7] This authority does not replace or limit the authority of state or local public health officials to abate or order abatement of public health nuisances or imminent hazards.[8] It is likely that state or local officials could use either the public health nuisance or imminent hazard authority to ensure that property contaminated with a nuclear, biological, or chemical agent was cleaned up. So what distinguishes this power from those?

First, this power may be exercised only by the state health director. Second, the context in which the public health threat abatement power may be exercised is narrower—the state health director may exercise it only when

---

5. G.S. 130A-475(a)(2).

6. G.S. 130A-475(a)(3).

7. G.S. 130A-477.

8. G.S. 130A-19 (public health nuisance authority); 130A-20 (imminent hazard authority). These authorities may be exercised by a local health director, the state secretary of health and human services, or the state secretary of environmental quality.

he or she reasonably suspects a public health threat caused by bioterrorism. The public health nuisance and imminent hazard authorities are not limited to that context. Third, the standard for ordering abatement of a public health threat appears to be somewhat lower than the standard for ordering abatement of a public health nuisance or imminent hazard. The state health director may order abatement of a public health threat that merely *may* exist because of the contamination of property by a nuclear, biological or chemical agent. In contrast, abatement of a public health nuisance or imminent hazard may be ordered or undertaken only after a determination that the nuisance or hazard *does* exist. Also, to abate a public health threat, the state health director only needs to conclude that the situation is likely to cause an immediate *risk* to human life or an immediate *risk* of serious physical injury, illness, or adverse health effects. In contrast, an imminent hazard is defined as a situation that is likely to cause an immediate *threat* to human life or health, and a public health nuisance action may require evidence that a condition actually endangers the public health.

Powers over Persons and Animals

When the state health director reasonably suspects that there may be a public health threat caused by bioterrorism, he or she may require persons or animals to submit to tests or examinations or may limit freedom of movement, action, or access to contaminated areas by persons or animals.

Tests or Examinations

The state health director may require any person or animal to submit to examinations or tests to determine possible exposure to a nuclear, biological, or chemical agent.[9]

Limitations on Freedom of Movement, Action, or Access

The state health director may limit the freedom of movement or action of a person or animal that is contaminated with, or reasonably suspected of being contaminated with, a nuclear, biological, or chemical agent that may

---

9. G.S. 130A-475(a)(1).

be conveyed to others.[10] He or she may also limit access to (1) an area or facility that is housing people or animals whose movement or action has been limited or (2) an area or facility that is contaminated with (or reasonably suspected of being contaminated with) a nuclear, biological, or chemical agent. However, the state health director may not restrict the access of authorized health care, law enforcement, or EMS personnel to the premises when they are conducting their duties.[11] Further, he or she must consult with the state veterinarian in the Department of Agriculture and Consumer Services before applying any of these limitations to livestock or poultry.

Orders limiting access to contaminated places may not exceed 30 days. Likewise, orders limiting the freedom of movement of contaminated persons may not exceed 30 days.[12] However, the 30-day limitation does not apply to an order limiting freedom of action. The terms "freedom of movement," "freedom of action," and "freedom of access" are not defined in the bioterrorism laws, but they are the same terms that are used in the state's communicable disease laws. An order limiting *freedom of movement* is generally understood as an order that prohibits an individual from going somewhere. It may confine the person to a particular place, such as his or her home, or it may prohibit the person from going to a particular place, such as work or school. In contrast, an order limiting *freedom of action* limits specific behaviors but not the ability to move freely in society. An order

---

10. G.S. 130A-475(a)(4).

11. G.S. 130A-475(a)(5). The provision actually states, "Nothing in this subdivision shall be construed to restrict the access of authorized health care, law enforcement, or emergency medical services personnel to *quarantine* or *isolation* premises as necessary to conduct their duties." (emphasis added). The reference to quarantine and isolation in the bioterrorism context is confusing, as both of those terms are associated with statutory definitions in G.S. 130A-2 that confine them to the communicable disease context. The authority in this statute goes beyond communicable disease—embracing nuclear and chemical agents as well as biological agents (which may also be broader than "communicable") and extending to areas that are contaminated as well as to individuals who have been contaminated by nuclear, biological, or chemical agents (which is different from being infected by or exposed to a communicable disease or condition). It seems reasonable to assume that the legislature intended to preserve access to contaminated areas (or those housing contaminated persons) for authorized health care, law enforcement, and EMS personnel, and that the use of the terms quarantine and isolation reflects colloquial rather than statutory definitions.

12. G.S. 130A-475(b).

limiting *freedom of access* prohibits a person from obtaining access to a designated place.

If the state health director determines that a limitation on freedom of movement or access must extend beyond 30 days, he or she must ask a superior court to order an extension. If the court determines that continued limitation is necessary to prevent or limit the conveyance of nuclear, biological, or chemical agents to others, the court will continue the limitation for up to 30 days. If necessary, the state health director may seek additional continuations of up to 30 days each.

A person who is substantially affected by an order limiting freedom of movement or access need not wait 30 days to obtain a superior court's review. He or she may ask a superior court to review the limitation, and the court must respond by holding a hearing within 72 hours (excluding Saturdays and Sundays). A person who seeks a court's review is entitled to representation by counsel and will receive appointed representation if he or she is indigent. If, after the hearing, the court determines by a preponderance of the evidence that the limitation on freedom of movement or access is not necessary to prevent or limit the conveyance of nuclear, biological, or chemical agents to others, the court must reduce the limitation. The court may also apply conditions to a limitation that the court deems reasonable and necessary.

Appendixes

Appendix 1

Communicable Disease Law Glossary

Communicable disease control has its own vocabulary. Many of the terms public health officials use have common meanings or medical definitions in addition to the legal definitions provided here. However, the statutory and regulatory definitions that follow are the ones that apply to the practice of communicable disease control by public health officials in North Carolina.

Bloodborne pathogens: "microorganisms that are present in human blood and can cause disease in humans." 29 C.F.R. § 1910.1030(b). The bloodborne pathogens addressed by OSHA standards and North Carolina communicable disease laws are human immunodeficiency virus (HIV), hepatitis B virus (HBV), and hepatitis C virus (HCV).

Communicable condition: "the state of being infected with a communicable agent but without symptoms." G.S. 130A-2(1b).

Communicable disease: "an illness due to an infectious agent or its toxic products which is transmitted directly or indirectly to a person from an infected person or animal through the agency of an intermediate animal, host, or vector, or through the inanimate environment." G.S. 130A-2(1c).

Health care–associated infection: "a localized or systemic condition in the patient resulting from an adverse reaction to the presence of an infectious agent(s) or its toxin(s) with no evidence that the infection was present or incubating when the patient was admitted to the health care setting." 10A N.C.A.C. 41A .0106(a)(3).

Household contact: "any person residing in the same domicile as the infected person." 10A N.C.A.C. 41A .0201(g).

Isolation authority: "the authority to issue an order to limit the freedom of movement or freedom of action of persons or animals that are infected or reasonably suspected to be infected with a communicable disease or communicable condition for the period of communicability to prevent the direct or indirect conveyance of the infectious agent from the person or animal to other persons or animals who are susceptible or who may spread the agent to others." G.S. 130A-2(3a).

Local health director: the administrative head of a county health department, a multi-county district health department, a consolidated human services agency that includes public health, or a public health authority; or the person within a consolidated human services agency to whom local health director powers and duties have been delegated. *See* G.S. 130A-2, 130A-43, 130A-45.4, 153A-77.

Notifiable disease or condition: a disease or condition that is included in the Centers for Disease Control and Prevention's (CDC) National Notifiable Diseases Surveillance System. The CDC designates the diseases and conditions that are notifiable, and states voluntarily provide case reports (without personal identifiers) for the system. *See* https://wwwn.cdc.gov/nndss/.

Other potentially infectious materials (OPIM): "(1) The following human body fluids: semen, vaginal secretions, cerebrospinal fluid, synovial fluid, pleural fluid, peritoneal fluid, amniotic fluid, saliva in dental procedures, any body fluid that is visibly contaminated with blood, and all body fluids in situations where it is difficult or impossible to differentiate between body fluids; (2) Any unfixed tissue or organ (other than intact skin) from a human (living or dead); and (3) HIV-containing cell or tissue cultures, organ cultures, and HIV- or HBV-containing culture medium or other solutions; and blood, organs, or other tissues from experimental animals infected with HIV or HBV." 29 C.F.R. § 1910.1030(b).

Outbreak: "an occurrence of a case or cases of a disease in a locale in excess of the usual number of cases of the disease." G.S. 130A-2(6a).

Personal protective equipment: "specialized clothing or equipment worn by an employee for protection against a hazard. General work clothes (e.g., uniforms, pants, shirts or blouses) not intended to function as protection against a hazard are not considered to be personal protective equipment." 29 C.F.R. § 1910.1030(b).

Quarantine authority: "the authority to issue an order to limit the freedom of movement or action of persons or animals which have been exposed to or are reasonably suspected of having been exposed to a communicable disease or communicable condition for a period of time as may be necessary to prevent the spread of that disease. Quarantine authority also means the authority to issue an order to limit access by any person or animal to an area or facility that may be contaminated with an infectious agent. The term also means the authority to issue an order to limit the freedom of movement or action of persons who have not received immunizations against a communicable disease when the State Health Director or a local health director determines that the immunizations are required to control an outbreak of that disease." G.S. 130A-2(7a).

Reportable disease or condition: a disease or condition that must be reported to public health officials by physicians or designated others. *See* G.S. 130A-134; 10A N.C.A.C. 41A .0101.

State health director: a North Carolina–licensed physician who is appointed by the state secretary of health and human services to carry out powers and duties determined by the secretary. G.S. 130A-3. The state health director also has a number of specific statutory powers and duties, including several related to communicable disease control.

Universal precautions: "an approach to infection control . . . [in which] all human blood and certain human body fluids are treated as if known to be infectious for HIV, HBV, and other bloodborne pathogens." 29 C.F.R. § 1910.1030(b).

Appendix 2

Index of North Carolina Communicable Disease Statutes and Rules, by Topic

Topic	Statutes (G.S.)	Rules (10A N.C.A.C.)
Generally Applicable		
Definitions of communicable disease terms	130A-2	
Delegation of authority	130A-6	
Powers and duties of a local health director	130A-41	
Enforcement/Public Health Remedies		
Injunction (civil remedy)	130A-18	
Misdemeanor (criminal remedy)	130A-25	
Reporting Communicable Diseases		
Establishing reportable diseases	130A-134	41A .0101
Persons authorized or required to report:		
• Physicians	130A-135	41A .0101(a), (b)
• School principals/child care operators	130A-136	41A .0101(a)
• Medical facilities	130A-137	41A .0101(a)
• Operators of restaurants/food and drink establishments	130A-138	41A .0102(b), (c)
• Persons in charge of laboratories	130A-139	41A .0101(c), 41A .0102(d), 41A .0209
• Local health directors	130A-140	41A .0103
• Temporary orders to report	130A-141.1	
Form, content, and timing of report	130A-141	41A .0101, 41A .0102
Immunity from liability for good faith reports	130A-142	
Health care–associated infections	130A-150	41A .0106
Reports associated with bioterrorism	130A-475	

(continued)

Topic	Statutes (G.S.)	Rules (10A N.C.A.C.)
Communicable Disease Investigations		
General provisions	130A-144(a)	41A .0103
Local health director's duty to investigate	130A-41(b)(3), (b)(8), & (b)(9); 130A-144(a)	
Access to information held by health care providers, laboratories, and other persons	130A-144(b)	
Immunity from liability for providing access to information	130A-144(c)	
Communicable Disease Control Measures		
In general		41A .0201
Duties of attending physician	130A-144(d)	41A .0210
Duties of local health director	130A-144(e)	41A .0103
Specific diseases/conditions		
• HIV/AIDS		41A .0202
• Hepatitis B		41A .0203
• Sexually transmitted diseases		41A .0204
• Tuberculosis		41A .0205
• Smallpox and vaccinia disease		41A .0208
• SARS		41A .0213
• Hepatitis C		41A .0214
• All others		41A .0201(a) & (b)
Individual's duty to comply with control measures	130A-144(f)	
Local health director's duty to ensure control measures are given	130A-144(e)	
Communicable Disease Confidentiality		
State communicable disease confidentiality law	G.S. 130A-143	
Access to information held by health care providers or laboratories	130A-144(b)	
Isolation and Quarantine		
In general	130A-145	
Local health director authority to order	130A-41(b)(4); 130A-145(a)	
State health director authority to order	130A-145(a)	
Restrictions on orders		41A .0201(d)

(continued)

Topic	Statutes (G.S.)	Rules (10A N.C.A.C.)
Due process provisions for orders limiting freedom of movement or access	130A-145(d)	
Detention of individuals who violate orders limiting freedom of movement or access	15A-401(b)(4); 15A-534.5	
Bloodborne Pathogens		
Basic rules	G.S. 130A-144	41A .0202(4); 41A .0203(b)(3) 41A .0214(4)
Determining significant risk of transmission		41A .0201(f)
Criminal defendants	15A-534.3	
Testing sex offenders	15A-615	
Bioterrorism		
All provisions	130A-475 through -479	

Appendix 3

Selected North Carolina General Statutes

Note: This compilation of statutes was up to date through the end of the 2016 legislative session. Please consult the official statutes to ensure that you are relying upon the most recent version of the law.

Definitions

§ 130A-2. Definitions.

The following definitions shall apply throughout this Chapter unless otherwise specified:

(1) "Accreditation board" or "Board" means the Local Health Department Accreditation Board.

(1a) "Commission" means the Commission for Public Health.

(1b) "Communicable condition" means the state of being infected with a communicable agent but without symptoms.

(1c) "Communicable disease" means an illness due to an infectious agent or its toxic products which is transmitted directly or indirectly to a person from an infected person or animal through the agency of an intermediate animal, host, or vector, or through the inanimate environment.

(2) "Department" means the Department of Health and Human Services.

(3) "Imminent hazard" means a situation that is likely to cause an immediate threat to human life, an immediate threat of serious physical injury, an immediate threat of serious adverse health effects, or a serious risk of irreparable damage to the environment if no immediate action is taken.

(3a) "Isolation authority" means the authority to issue an order to limit the freedom of movement or action of persons or animals that are infected or reasonably suspected to be infected with a communicable disease or communicable condition for the period of communicability to prevent the direct or indirect conveyance of the infectious agent from the person or animal to other persons or animals who are susceptible or who may spread the agent to others.

(4) "Local board of health" means a district board of health or a public health authority board or a county board of health.

(5) "Local health department" means a district health department or a public health authority or a county health department.

(6) "Local health director" means the administrative head of a local health department appointed pursuant to this Chapter.

(6a) "Outbreak" means an occurrence of a case or cases of a disease in a locale in excess of the usual number of cases of the disease.

(7) "Person" means an individual, corporation, company, association, partnership, unit of local government or other legal entity.

(7a) "Quarantine authority" means the authority to issue an order to limit the freedom of movement or action of persons or animals which have been exposed to or are reasonably suspected of having been exposed to a communicable disease or communicable condition for a period of time as may be necessary to prevent the spread of that disease. Quarantine authority also means the authority to issue an order to limit access by any person or animal to an area or facility that may be contaminated with an infectious agent. The term also means the authority to issue an order to limit the freedom of movement or action of persons who have not received immunizations against a communicable disease when the State Health Director or a local health director determines that the immunizations are required to control an outbreak of that disease.

(8) "Secretary" means the Secretary of Health and Human Services.

(9) "Unit of local government" means a county, city, consolidated city-county, sanitary district or other local political subdivision, authority or agency of local government.

(10) "Vital records" means birth, death, fetal death, marriage, annulment and divorce records registered under the provisions of Article 4 of this Chapter.

Delegation of Authority

§ 130A-6. Delegation of authority.

Whenever authority is granted by this Chapter upon a public official, the authority may be delegated to another person authorized by the public official.

Remedies

§ 130A-18. Injunction.

(a) If a person shall violate any provision of this Chapter, the rules adopted by the Commission or rules adopted by a local board of health, or a condition or term of a permit or order issued under this Chapter, the Secretary or a local health director may institute an action for injunctive relief, irrespective of all other remedies at law, in the superior court of the county where the violation occurred or where a defendant resides.

(b) The Secretary of Environmental Quality and a local health director shall have the same rights enumerated in subsection (a) of this section to enforce the provisions of Articles 9 and 10 of this Chapter.

§ 130A-25. Misdemeanor.

(a) Except as otherwise provided, a person who violates a provision of this Chapter or the rules adopted by the Commission or a local board of health shall be guilty of a misdemeanor.

(b) A person convicted under this section for violation of G.S. 130A-144(f) or G.S. 130A-145 shall not be sentenced under Article 81B of Chapter 15A of the General Statutes but shall instead be sentenced to a term of imprisonment of no more than two years and shall serve any prison sentence in McCain Hospital, Section of Prisons of the Division of Adult Correction, McCain, North Carolina; the North Carolina Correctional Center for Women, Section of Prisons of the Division of Adult Correction, Raleigh, North Carolina; or any other confinement facility designated for this purpose by the Secretary of Public Safety after consultation with the State Health Director. The Secretary of Public Safety shall consult with the State Health Director concerning the medical management of these persons.

(c) Notwithstanding G.S. 148-4.1, G.S. 148-13, or any other contrary provision of law, a person imprisoned for violation of G.S. 130A-144(f) or G.S. 130A-145 shall not be released prior to the completion of the person's term of imprisonment unless and until a determination has been made by the District Court that release of the person would not create a danger to the public health. This determination shall be made only after the medical consultant of the confinement facility and the State Health Director, in consultation with the local health director of the person's county of residence, have made recommendations to the Court.

(d) A violation of Part 7 of Article 9 of this Chapter or G.S. 130A-309.10(m) shall be punishable as a Class 3 misdemeanor.

Local Health Director Powers and Duties

§ 130A-41. Powers and duties of local health director.

(a) A local health director shall be the administrative head of the local health department, shall perform public health duties prescribed by and under the supervision of the local board of health and the Department and shall be employed full time in the field of public health.

(b) A local health director shall have the following powers and duties:

(1) To administer programs as directed by the local board of health;

(2) To enforce the rules of the local board of health;

(3) To investigate the causes of infectious, communicable and other diseases;

(4) To exercise quarantine authority and isolation authority pursuant to G.S. 130A-145;

(5) To disseminate public health information and to promote the benefits of good health;

(6) To advise local officials concerning public health matters;

(7) To enforce the immunization requirements of Part 2 of Article 6 of this Chapter;

(8) To examine and investigate cases of venereal disease pursuant to Parts 3 and 4 of Article 6 of this Chapter;

(9) To examine and investigate cases of tuberculosis pursuant to Part 5 of Article 6 of this Chapter;

(10) To examine, investigate and control rabies pursuant to Part 6 of Article 6 of this Chapter;

(11) To abate public health nuisances and imminent hazards pursuant to G.S. 130A-19 and G.S. 130A-20;

(12) To employ and dismiss employees of the local health department in accordance with Chapter 126 of the General Statutes;

(13) To enter contracts, in accordance with The Local Government Finance Act, G.S. Chapter 159, on behalf of the local health department. Nothing in this paragraph shall be construed to abrogate the authority of the board of county commissioners.

(c) Authority conferred upon a local health director may be exercised only within the county or counties comprising the local health department.

Communicable Disease Control
Article 6.
Communicable Diseases.
Part 1. In General.

§ 130A-133: Repealed by Session Laws 2002-179, s. 3, effective October 1, 2002.

§ 130A-134. Reportable diseases and conditions.
The Commission shall establish by rule a list of communicable diseases and communicable conditions to be reported.

§ 130A-135. Physicians to report.
A physician licensed to practice medicine who has reason to suspect that a person about whom the physician has been consulted professionally has a communicable disease or communicable condition declared by the Commission to be reported, shall report information required by the Commission to the local health director of the county or district in which

the physician is consulted. The Commission shall declare confirmed HIV infection to be a reportable communicable condition.

§ 130A-136. School principals and child care operators to report.

A principal of a school and an operator of a child care facility, as defined in G.S. 110-86(3), who has reason to suspect that a person within the school or child care facility has a communicable disease or communicable condition declared by the Commission to be reported, shall report information required by the Commission to the local health director of the county or district in which the school or facility is located.

§ 130A-137. Medical facilities may report.

A medical facility, in which there is a patient reasonably suspected of having a communicable disease or condition declared by the Commission to be reported, may report information specified by the Commission to the local health director of the county or district in which the facility is located.

§ 130A-138. Operators of restaurants and other food or drink establishments to report.

An operator of a restaurant or other establishment where food or drink is prepared or served for pay, as defined in G.S. 130A-247(4) and (5), shall report information required by the Commission to the local health director of the county or district in which the restaurant or food establishment is located when the operator has reason to suspect an outbreak of food-borne illness in its customers or employees or when it has reason to suspect that a food handler at the establishment has a food-borne disease or food-borne condition required by the Commission to be reported.

§ 130A-139. Persons in charge of laboratories to report.

A person in charge of a laboratory providing diagnostic service in this State shall report information required by the Commission to a public health agency specified by the Commission when the laboratory makes any of the following findings:

    (1)   Sputa, gastric contents, or other specimens which are smear positive for acid fast bacilli or culture positive for Mycobacterium tuberculosis;

(2) Urethral smears positive for Gram-negative intracellular diplococci or any culture positive for Neisseria gonorrhoeae;

(3) Positive serological tests for syphilis or positive darkfield examination;

(4) Any other positive test indicative of a communicable disease or communicable condition for which laboratory reporting is required by the Commission.

§ 130A-140. Local health directors to report.

A local health director shall report to the Department all cases of diseases or conditions or laboratory findings of residents of the jurisdiction of the local health department which are reported to the local health director pursuant to this Article. A local health director shall report all other cases and laboratory findings reported pursuant to this Article to the local health director of the county, district, or authority where the person with the reportable disease or condition or laboratory finding resides.

§ 130A-141. Form, content and timing of reports.

The Commission shall adopt rules which establish the specific information to be submitted when making a report required by this Article, time limits for reporting, the form of the reports and to whom reports of laboratory findings are to be made.

§ 130A-141.1. Temporary order to report.

(a) The State Health Director may issue a temporary order requiring health care providers to report symptoms, diseases, conditions, trends in use of health care services, or other health-related information when necessary to conduct a public health investigation or surveillance of an illness, condition, or symptoms that may indicate the existence of a communicable disease or condition that presents a danger to the public health. The order shall specify which health care providers must report, what information is to be reported, and the period of time for which reporting is required. The period of time for which reporting is required pursuant to a temporary order shall not exceed 90 days. The Commission may adopt rules to continue the reporting requirement when necessary to protect the public health.

(b) For the purposes of this section, the term "health care provider" has the same meaning as that term is defined in G.S. 130A-476(g).

§ 130A-142. Immunity of persons who report.

A person who makes a report pursuant to the provisions of this Article shall be immune from any civil or criminal liability that might otherwise be incurred or imposed as a result of making that report.

§ 130A-143. Confidentiality of records.

All information and records, whether publicly or privately maintained, that identify a person who has AIDS virus infection or who has or may have a disease or condition required to be reported pursuant to the provisions of this Article shall be strictly confidential. This information shall not be released or made public except under the following circumstances:

(1) Release is made of specific medical or epidemiological information for statistical purposes in a way that no person can be identified;

(2) Release is made of all or part of the medical record with the written consent of the person or persons identified or their guardian;

(3) Release is made for purposes of treatment, payment, research, or health care operations to the extent that disclosure is permitted under 45 Code of Federal Regulations §§ 164.506 and 164.512(i). For purposes of this section, the terms "treatment," "payment," "research," and "health care operations" have the meaning given those terms in 45 Code of Federal Regulations § 164.501;

(4) Release is necessary to protect the public health and is made as provided by the Commission in its rules regarding control measures for communicable diseases and conditions;

(5) Release is made pursuant to other provisions of this Article;

(6) Release is made pursuant to subpoena or court order. Upon request of the person identified in the record, the record shall be reviewed in camera. In the trial, the trial judge may, during the taking of testimony concerning such information, exclude from the courtroom all persons except the officers of the court, the parties and those engaged in the trial of the case;

(7) Release is made by the Department or a local health department to a court or a law enforcement official for the purpose

of enforcing this Article or Article 22 of this Chapter, or investigating a terrorist incident using nuclear, biological, or chemical agents. A law enforcement official who receives the information shall not disclose it further, except (i) when necessary to enforce this Article or Article 22 of this Chapter, or when necessary to conduct an investigation of a terrorist incident using nuclear, biological, or chemical agents, or (ii) when the Department or a local health department seeks the assistance of the law enforcement official in preventing or controlling the spread of the disease or condition and expressly authorizes the disclosure as necessary for that purpose;

(8) Release is made by the Department or a local health department to another federal, state or local public health agency for the purpose of preventing or controlling the spread of a communicable disease or communicable condition;

(9) Release is made by the Department for bona fide research purposes. The Commission shall adopt rules providing for the use of the information for research purposes;

(10) Release is made pursuant to G.S. 130A-144(b); or

(11) Release is made pursuant to any other provisions of law that specifically authorize or require the release of information or records related to AIDS.

§ 130A-144. Investigation and control measures.

(a) The local health director shall investigate, as required by the Commission, cases of communicable diseases and communicable conditions reported to the local health director pursuant to this Article.

(b) Physicians, persons in charge of medical facilities or laboratories, and other persons shall, upon request and proper identification, permit a local health director or the State Health Director to examine, review, and obtain a copy of medical or other records in their possession or under their control which the State Health Director or a local health director determines pertain to the (i) diagnosis, treatment, or prevention of a communicable disease or communicable condition for a person infected, exposed, or reasonably suspected of being infected or exposed to such a disease or condition, or (ii) the investigation of a known or reasonably suspected outbreak of a communicable disease or communicable condition.

(c) A physician or a person in charge of a medical facility or laboratory who permits examination, review or copying of medical records pursuant to subsection (b) shall be immune from any civil or criminal liability that otherwise might be incurred or imposed as a result of complying with a request made pursuant to subsection (b).

(d) The attending physician shall give control measures prescribed by the Commission to a patient with a communicable disease or communicable condition and to patients reasonably suspected of being infected or exposed to such a disease or condition. The physician shall also give control measures to other individuals as required by rules adopted by the Commission.

(e) The local health director shall ensure that control measures prescribed by the Commission have been given to prevent the spread of all reportable communicable diseases or communicable conditions and any other communicable disease or communicable condition that represents a significant threat to the public health. The local health department shall provide, at no cost to the patient, the examination and treatment for tuberculosis disease and infection and for sexually transmitted diseases designated by the Commission.

(f) All persons shall comply with control measures, including submission to examinations and tests, prescribed by the Commission subject to the limitations of G.S. 130A-148.

(g) The Commission shall adopt rules that prescribe control measures for communicable diseases and conditions subject to the limitations of G.S. 130A-148. Temporary rules prescribing control measures for communicable diseases and conditions shall be adopted pursuant to G.S. 150B-13.

(h) Anyone who assists in an inquiry or investigation conducted by the State Health Director for the purpose of evaluating the risk of transmission of HIV or Hepatitis B from an infected health care worker to patients, or who serves on an expert panel established by the State Health Director for that purpose, shall be immune from civil liability that otherwise might be incurred or imposed for any acts or omissions which result from such assistance or service, provided that the person acts in good faith and the acts or omissions do not amount to gross negligence, willful or wanton misconduct, or intentional wrongdoing. This qualified immunity does not apply to acts or omissions which occur with respect to the operation of a motor vehicle. Nothing in this subsection provides immunity from liability for a violation of G.S. 130A-143.

§ 130A-145. Quarantine and isolation authority.

(a) The State Health Director and a local health director are empowered to exercise quarantine and isolation authority. Quarantine and isolation authority shall be exercised only when and so long as the public health is endangered, all other reasonable means for correcting the problem have been exhausted, and no less restrictive alternative exists.

(b) No person other than a person authorized by the State Health Director or local health director shall enter quarantine or isolation premises. Nothing in this subsection shall be construed to restrict the access of authorized health care, law enforcement, or emergency medical services personnel to quarantine or isolation premises as necessary in conducting their duties.

(c) Before applying quarantine or isolation authority to livestock or poultry for the purpose of preventing the direct or indirect conveyance of an infectious agent to persons, the State Health Director or a local health director shall consult with the State Veterinarian in the Department of Agriculture and Consumer Services.

(d) When quarantine or isolation limits the freedom of movement of a person or animal or of access to a person or animal whose freedom of movement is limited, the period of limited freedom of movement or access shall not exceed 30 calendar days. Any person substantially affected by that limitation may institute in superior court in Wake County or in the county in which the limitation is imposed an action to review that limitation. The official who exercises the quarantine or isolation authority shall give the persons known by the official to be substantially affected by the limitation reasonable notice under the circumstances of the right to institute an action to review the limitation. If a person or a person's representative requests a hearing, the hearing shall be held within 72 hours of the filing of that request, excluding Saturdays and Sundays. The person substantially affected by that limitation is entitled to be represented by counsel of the person's own choice or if the person is indigent, the person shall be represented by counsel appointed in accordance with Article 36 of Chapter 7A of the General Statutes and the rules adopted by the Office of Indigent Defense Services. The court shall reduce or terminate the limitation unless it determines, by the preponderance of the evidence, that the limitation is reasonably necessary to prevent or limit the conveyance of a communicable disease or condition to others.

If the State Health Director or the local health director determines that a 30-calendar-day limitation on freedom of movement or access is not adequate to protect the public health, the State Health Director or local health director must institute in superior court in the county in which the limitation is imposed an action to obtain an order extending the period of limitation of freedom of movement or access. If the person substantially affected by the limitation has already instituted an action in superior court in Wake County, the State Health Director must institute the action in superior court in Wake County or as a counterclaim in the pending case. Except as provided below for persons with tuberculosis, the court shall continue the limitation for a period not to exceed 30 days if it determines, by the preponderance of the evidence, that the limitation is reasonably necessary to prevent or limit the conveyance of a communicable disease or condition to others. The court order shall specify the period of time the limitation is to be continued and shall provide for automatic termination of the order upon written determination by the State Health Director or local health director that the quarantine or isolation is no longer necessary to protect the public health. In addition, where the petitioner can prove by a preponderance of the evidence that quarantine or isolation was not or is no longer needed for protection of the public health, the person quarantined or isolated may move the trial court to reconsider its order extending quarantine or isolation before the time for the order otherwise expires and may seek immediate or expedited termination of the order. Before the expiration of an order issued under this section, the State Health Director or local health director may move to continue the order for additional periods not to exceed 30 days each. If the person whose freedom of movement has been limited has tuberculosis, the court shall continue the limitation for a period not to exceed one calendar year if it determines, by a preponderance of the evidence, that the limitation is reasonably necessary to prevent or limit the conveyance of tuberculosis to others. The court order shall specify the period of time the limitation is to be continued and shall provide for automatic termination of the order upon written determination by the State Health Director or local health director that the quarantine or isolation is no longer necessary to protect the public health. In addition, where the petitioner can prove by a preponderance of the evidence that quarantine or isolation was not or is no longer needed for protection of the public health, the person quarantined or isolated may move the trial court to reconsider its order extending quarantine or isolation before the time for the order otherwise expires and may seek immediate or expedited termination of the order. Before the expiration of an order limiting the freedom of movement of a person with tuberculosis, the State Health Director or local health director may move to continue the order for additional periods not to exceed one calendar year each.

§ 130A-146. Transportation of bodies of persons who have died of reportable diseases.

No person shall transport in this State the remains of any person who has died of a disease declared by the Commission to be reported until the body has been encased in a manner as prescribed by rule by the Commission. Only persons who have complied with the rules of the Commission concerning the removal of dead bodies shall be issued a burial-transit permit.

§ 130A-147. Rules of the Commission.

For the protection of the public health, the Commission is authorized to adopt rules for the detection, control and prevention of communicable diseases.

§ 130A-148. Laboratory tests for AIDS virus infection.

(a) For the protection of the public health, the Commission shall adopt rules establishing standards for the certification of laboratories to perform tests for Acquired Immune Deficiency Syndrome (AIDS) virus infection. The rules shall address, but not be limited to, proficiency testing, record maintenance, adequate staffing and confirmatory testing. Tests for AIDS virus infection shall be performed only by laboratories certified pursuant to this subsection and only on specimens submitted by a physician licensed to practice medicine. This subsection shall not apply to testing performed solely for research purposes under the approval of an institutional review board.

(b) Prior to obtaining consent for donation of blood, semen, tissue or organs, a facility or institution seeking to obtain blood, tissue, semen or organs for transfusion, implantation, transplantation or administration shall provide the potential donor with information about AIDS virus transmission, and information about who should not donate.

(c) No blood or semen may be transfused or administered when blood from the donor has not been tested or has tested positive for AIDS virus infection by a standard laboratory test.

(d) No tissue or organs may be transplanted or implanted when blood from the donor has not been tested or has tested positive for AIDS virus infection by a standard laboratory test unless consent is obtained from the recipient, or from the recipient's guardian or a responsible adult relative of the recipient if the recipient is not competent to give such consent.

(e) Any facility or institution that obtains or transfuses, implants, transplants, or administers blood, tissue, semen, or organs shall be immune from civil or criminal liability that otherwise might be incurred or imposed for transmission of AIDS virus infection if the provisions specified in subsections (b), (c), and (d) of this section have been complied with.

(f) Specimens may be tested for AIDS virus infection for research or epidemiologic purposes without consent of the person from whom the specimen is obtained if all personal identifying information is removed from the specimen prior to testing.

(g) Persons tested for AIDS virus infection shall be notified of test results and counseled appropriately. This subsection shall not apply to tests performed by or for entities governed by Article 39 of Chapter 58 of the General Statutes, the Insurance Information and Privacy Protection Act, provided that said entities comply with the notice requirements thereof.

(h) The Commission may authorize or require laboratory tests for AIDS virus infection when necessary to protect the public health.

A test for AIDS virus infection may also be performed upon any person solely by order of a physician licensed to practice medicine in North Carolina who is rendering medical services to that person when, in the reasonable medical judgment of the physician, the test is necessary for the appropriate treatment of the person; however, the person shall be informed that a test for AIDS virus infection is to be conducted, and shall be given clear opportunity to refuse to submit to the test prior to it being conducted, and further if informed consent is not obtained, the test may not be performed. A physician may order a test for AIDS virus infection without the informed consent of the person tested if the person is incapable of providing or incompetent to provide such consent, others authorized to give consent for the person are not available, and testing is necessary for appropriate diagnosis or care of the person.

An unemancipated minor may be tested for AIDS virus infection without the consent of the parent or legal guardian of the minor when the parent or guardian has refused to consent to such testing and there is reasonable suspicion that the minor has AIDS virus or HIV infection or that the child has been sexually abused.

(i) Except as provided in this section, no test for AIDS virus infection shall be required, performed or used to determine suitability for continued employment, housing or public services, or for the use of places of public accommodation as defined in G.S. 168A-3(8), or public transportation.

Further it shall be unlawful to discriminate against any person having AIDS virus or HIV infection on account of that infection in determining suitability for continued employment, housing, or public services, or for the use of places of public accommodation, as defined in G.S. 168A-3(8), or public transportation.

Any person aggrieved by an act or discriminatory practice prohibited by this subsection relating to housing shall be entitled to institute a civil action pursuant to G.S. 41A-7 of the State Fair Housing Act. Any person aggrieved by an act or discriminatory practice prohibited by this subsection other than one relating to housing may bring a civil action to enforce rights granted or protected by this subsection.

The action shall be commenced in superior court in the county where the alleged discriminatory practice or prohibited conduct occurred or where the plaintiff or defendant resides. Such action shall be tried to the court without a jury. Any relief granted by the court shall be limited to declaratory and injunctive relief, including orders to hire or reinstate an aggrieved person or admit such person to a labor organization.

In a civil action brought to enforce provisions of this subsection relating to employment, the court may award back pay. Any such back pay liability shall not accrue from a date more than two years prior to the filing of an action under this subsection. Interim earnings or amounts earnable with reasonable diligence by the aggrieved person shall operate to reduce the back pay otherwise allowable. In any civil action brought under this subsection, the court, in its discretion, may award reasonable attorney's fees to the substantially prevailing party as a part of costs.

A civil action brought pursuant to this subsection shall be commenced within 180 days after the date on which the aggrieved person became aware or, with reasonable diligence, should have become aware of the alleged discriminatory practice or prohibited conduct.

Nothing in this section shall be construed so as to prohibit an employer from:

(1) Requiring a test for AIDS virus infection for job applicants in preemployment medical examinations required by the employer;

(2) Denying employment to a job applicant based solely on a confirmed positive test for AIDS virus infection;

(3) Including a test for AIDS virus infection performed in the course of an annual medical examination routinely required of all employees by the employer; or

(4) Taking the appropriate employment action, including reassignment or termination of employment, if the continuation by the employee who has AIDS virus or HIV infection of his work tasks would pose a significant risk to the health of the employee, coworkers, or the public, or if the employee is unable to perform the normally assigned duties of the job.

(j) It shall not be unlawful for a licensed health care provider or facility to:

(1) Treat a person who has AIDS virus or HIV infection differently from persons who do not have that infection when such treatment is appropriate to protect the health care provider or employees of the provider or employees of the facility while providing appropriate care for the person who has the AIDS virus or HIV infection; or

(2) Refer a person who has AIDS virus or HIV infection to another licensed health care provider or facility when such referral is for the purpose of providing more appropriate treatment for the person with AIDS virus or HIV infection.

§ 130A-149: Recodified as G.S. 130A-479 by Session Laws 2002-179, s. 2, effective October 1, 2002.

Part 1A. Health Care-Associated Infections.

§ 130A-150. Statewide surveillance and reporting system.

(a) By December 31, 2011, the Department, in consultation with the State HAI Advisory Group and in accordance with rules adopted by the Commission pursuant to subsection (b) of this section, shall establish a statewide surveillance and reporting system for specified health care-associated infections.

(b) The Commission shall adopt rules necessary to implement the statewide surveillance and reporting system established pursuant to subsection (a) of this section. The rules shall specify uniform standards for surveillance and reporting of specified health care-associated infections under the statewide surveillance and reporting system. The uniform standards shall include at least all of the following:

(1) A preference for electronic surveillance of specified health care-associated infections to the greatest extent practicable.

(2) A requirement for electronic reporting of specified health care-associated infections.

(c) Each hospital, as defined in G.S. 131E-76(3), is subject to the statewide surveillance and reporting system established in accordance with subsection (a) of this section and shall be responsible for health care-associated infections surveillance and reporting of specified health care-associated infections data to the Department through the Centers for Disease Control and Prevention National Health Care Safety Network.

(d) The Department shall release to the public aggregated and provider-specific data on health care-associated infections that does not contain social security numbers or other personal identifying information only if it deems the release of this data to be reliable and necessary to protect the public's health.

(e) Repealed by Session Laws 2013-360, s. 12A.8(d), effective July 1, 2013.

§ 130A-151. Reserved for future codification purposes.

Public Health Bioterrorism
Article 22.
A Terrorist Incident Using Nuclear, Biological, or Chemical Agents.

§ 130A-475. Suspected terrorist attack.

(a) If the State Health Director reasonably suspects that a public health threat may exist and that the threat may have been caused by a terrorist incident using nuclear, biological, or chemical agents, the State Health Director is authorized to order any of the following:

(1) Require any person or animal to submit to examinations and tests to determine possible exposure to the nuclear, biological, or chemical agents.

(2) Test any real or personal property necessary to determine the presence of nuclear, biological, or chemical agents.

(3) Evacuate or close any real property, including any building, structure, or land when necessary to investigate suspected contamination of the property. The period of closure during an investigation shall not exceed 10 calendar days. If the State Health Director determines that a longer period of closure is necessary to complete the investigation, the Director may institute an action in superior court to order the property to remain closed until the investigation is completed.

(4) Limit the freedom of movement or action of a person or animal that is contaminated with, or reasonably suspected of being contaminated with, a biological, chemical or nuclear agent that may be conveyed to other persons or animals.

(5) Limit access by any person or animal to an area or facility that is housing persons or animals whose movement or action has been limited under subdivision (4) of this subsection or to an area or facility that is contaminated with, or reasonably suspected of being contaminated with, a biological, chemical or nuclear agent that may be conveyed to other persons or animals. Nothing in this subdivision shall be construed to restrict the access of authorized health care, law enforcement, or emergency medical services personnel to quarantine or isolation premises as necessary in conducting their duties.

(b) The authority under subsection (a) of this section shall be exercised only when and so long as a public health threat may exist, all other reasonable means for correcting the problem have been exhausted, and no less restrictive alternative exists. Before applying the authority under subdivision (4) or (5) of subsection (a) of this section to livestock or poultry for the purpose of preventing the direct or indirect conveyance of a biological, chemical or nuclear agent to persons, the State Health Director shall consult with the State Veterinarian in the Department of Agriculture and Consumer Services.

The period of limited freedom of movement or access under subdivisions (4) and (5) of subsection (a) of this section shall not exceed 30 calendar days. Any person substantially affected by that limitation may institute, in superior court in Wake County or in the county in which the limitation is imposed, an action to review the limitation. The State Health Director shall give the persons known by the State Health Director to be substantially affected by the limitation reasonable notice under the circumstances of the right to institute an action to review the limitation. If a person or a person's representative requests a hearing, the hearing shall be held within 72 hours of the filing of the request, excluding Saturdays and Sundays. The person substantially affected by that limitation is entitled to be represented by counsel of the person's own choice or if the person is indigent, the person shall be represented by counsel appointed in accordance with Article 36 of Chapter 7A of the General Statutes and the rules adopted by the Office of Indigent Defense Services. The court shall reduce or terminate the limitation unless it determines, by the preponderance of the evidence, that the limitation is reasonably necessary to prevent or limit the conveyance of biological, chemical or nuclear agents to others, and may apply such conditions to the limitation as the court deems reasonable and necessary.

If the State Health Director determines that a 30-calendar-day limitation on freedom of movement or access is not adequate to protect the public health, the State Health Director must institute in superior court in the county in which the limitation is imposed, an action to obtain an order extending the period limiting the freedom of movement or access. If the person substantially affected by the limitation has already instituted an action in superior court in Wake County, the State Health Director must institute the action in superior court in Wake County or as a counterclaim in the pending case. The court shall continue the limitation for a period not to exceed 30 days, subject to conditions it deems reasonable and necessary, if it determines by the preponderance of the evidence, that additional limitation is reasonably necessary to prevent or limit the conveyance of biological, chemical, or nuclear agents to others. The court order shall specify the period of time the limitation is to be continued and shall provide for automatic termination of the order upon written determination by the State Health Director or local health director that the limitation on freedom of movement or access is no longer necessary to protect the public health. In addition, where the petitioner can prove by a preponderance of the evidence that the limitation on freedom of movement or access was not or is no longer needed for protection of the public health, the person so limited may move the trial court to reconsider its order extending the limitation on freedom of movement or access before the time for the order otherwise expires and may seek immediate or expedited termination of the order. Before the expiration of an order issued under this section, the State Health Director may move to continue the order for additional periods not to exceed 30 days each.

(c) If the State Health Director reasonably suspects that there exists a public health threat that may have been caused by a terrorist incident using nuclear, biological, or chemical agents, the State Health Director shall notify the Governor and the Secretary of Public Safety. If the Secretary of Public Safety reasonably suspects that a public health threat may exist and that the threat may have been caused by a terrorist incident using nuclear, biological, or chemical agents, the Secretary shall notify the Governor and the State Health Director.

(d) For the purpose of this Article, the term "public health threat" means a situation that is likely to cause an immediate risk to human life, an immediate risk of serious physical injury or illness, or an immediate risk of serious adverse health effects.

(e) Nothing in this section shall limit any authority otherwise granted to local or State public health officials under this Chapter.

§ 130A-476. Access to health information.

(a) Notwithstanding any other provision of law, a health care provider, a person in charge of a health care facility, or a unit of State or local government may report to the State Health Director or a local health director any events that may indicate the existence of a case or outbreak of an illness, condition, or health hazard that may have been caused by a terrorist incident using nuclear, biological, or chemical agents. Events that may be reported include unusual types or numbers of symptoms or illnesses presented to the provider, unusual trends in health care visits, or unusual trends in prescriptions or purchases of over-the-counter pharmaceuticals. To the extent practicable, a person who makes a report under this subsection shall not disclose personally identifiable information. A person disclosing or not disclosing information pursuant to this subsection is immune from any civil or criminal liability that might otherwise be incurred or imposed based on the disclosure or lack of disclosure provided that the health care provider was acting in good faith and without malice. In any proceeding involving liability, good faith and lack of malice are presumed. Notwithstanding the foregoing, if a health care provider or unit of State or local government willfully does not disclose information pursuant to this subsection, the immunity from civil or criminal liability provided under this subsection shall not be available if the person had actual knowledge that a condition or illness was caused by use of a nuclear, biological, or chemical weapon of mass destruction as defined in G.S. 14-288.21(c).

(b) The State Health Director may issue a temporary order requiring health care providers to report symptoms, diseases, conditions, trends in use of health care services, or other health-related information when necessary to conduct a public health investigation or surveillance of an illness, condition, or health hazard that may have been caused by a terrorist incident using nuclear, biological, or chemical agents. The order shall specify which health care providers must report, what information is to be reported, and the period of time for which reporting is required. The period of time for which reporting is required pursuant to a temporary order shall not exceed 90 days. The Commission may adopt rules to continue the reporting requirement when necessary to protect the public health.

(c) Health care providers and persons in charge of health care facilities or laboratories shall, upon request and proper identification, permit the State Health Director or a local health director to examine, review, and obtain a copy of records containing confidential or protected health information, or a summary of pertinent portions of those records, (i) that pertain to a report authorized by subsection (a) or required by subsection (b) of this section, or (ii) that, in the opinion of the State Health Director or local health director, are necessary for an investigation of a case or outbreak of an illness, condition, or health hazard that may have been caused by a terrorist incident using nuclear, biological, or chemical agents.

(d) A person who makes a report pursuant to subsection (b) of this section or permits examination, review, or copying of medical records pursuant to subsection (c) of this section is immune from any civil or criminal liability that otherwise might be incurred or imposed as a result of complying with those subsections.

(e) Confidential or protected health information received by the State Health Director or a local health director pursuant to this section shall be confidential and shall not be released, except when the release is:

(1) Made pursuant to any other provision of law;

(2) To another federal, state, or local public health agency for the purpose of preventing or controlling a public health threat; or

(3) To a court or law enforcement official or law enforcement officer for the purpose of enforcing the provisions of this Chapter or for the purpose of investigating a terrorist incident using nuclear, biological, or chemical agents. A court or law enforcement official or law enforcement officer who receives the information shall not disclose it further, except (i) when necessary to conduct an investigation of a terrorist incident using nuclear, biological, or chemical agents, or (ii) when the State Health Director or a local health director seeks the assistance of the court or law enforcement official or law enforcement officer in preventing or controlling the public health threat and expressly authorizes the disclosure as necessary for that purpose.

(f) Repealed by Session Laws 2004-124, s. 10.34(a), effective January 1, 2005.

(g) In this section the following terms shall include:

(1) "Health care provider" includes a physician licensed to practice medicine in North Carolina or a person who is licensed, certified, or credentialed to practice or provide health care services, including, but not limited to, pharmacists, dentists, physician assistants, registered nurses, licensed practical nurses, advanced practice nurses, chiropractors, respiratory care therapists, and emergency medical technicians; and

(2) "Health care facility" includes hospitals, skilled nursing facilities, intermediate care facilities, psychiatric facilities, rehabilitation facilities, home health agencies, ambulatory surgical facilities, or any other health care related facility, whether publicly or privately owned.

§ 130A-477. Abatement of public health threat.

If it is determined that a public health threat may exist because of the contamination of property caused by a terrorist incident using nuclear, biological, or chemical agents, the State Health Director may order any action to abate that public health threat. To the extent that any owner, lessee, operator, or other person in control of the property is innocent of culpability in the creation of the public health threat, that person shall not be responsible for the costs of abating the public health threat.

§ 130A-478. Tort liability.

Article 31 of Chapter 143 applies to negligent acts committed by any officer, employee, involuntary servant or agent of the State acting pursuant to this Article.

§ 130A-479. Biological agents registry; rules; penalties.

(a) The Department shall establish and administer a program for the registration of biological agents. The biological agents registry shall identify the biological agents possessed and maintained by any person in this State and shall contain other information required under rules adopted by the Commission.

(b) The following definitions apply in this section:

(1) "Biological agent" means:

a. Any select agent that is a microorganism, virus, bacterium, fungus, rickettsia, or toxin listed in Appendix A of Part 72 of Title 42 of the Code of Federal Regulations.

b. Any genetically modified microorganisms or genetic elements from an organism on Appendix A of Part 72 of Title 42 of the Code of Federal Regulations, shown to produce or encode for a factor associated with a disease.

c. Any genetically modified microorganisms or genetic elements that contain nucleic acid sequences coding for any of the toxins listed on Appendix A of Part 72 of Title 42 of the Code of Federal Regulations, or their toxic submits.

(2) "Person" means any association, business, corporation, facility, firm, individual, institution of higher education, organization, partnership, society, State agency, or other legal entity.

(c) The Commission shall adopt rules for the implementation of the registry program, as follows:

(1) Determining and listing the biological agents required to be reported under this section.

(2) Designating persons required to make reports and specific information required to be reported including time limits for reporting, form of reports, and to whom reports shall be submitted.

(3) Providing for the release of information in the registry to State and federal law enforcement agencies and the United States Centers for Disease Control and Prevention pursuant to a communicable disease investigation commenced or conducted by the Department, the Commission, or other state or federal law enforcement agency having investigatory authority, or in connection with any investigation involving release, theft, or loss of biological agents.

(4) Establishing a system of safeguards that requires persons possessing and maintaining biological agents subject to this section to comply with the same federal standards that apply to persons registered to possess the same agents under federal law.

(5) Establishing a process for persons that possess and maintain biological agents to alert appropriate authorities of unauthorized possession or attempted possession of biological agents. The rules shall designate appropriate authorities for receipt of alerts from these persons.

(d) Any person that possesses and maintains any biological agent required to be reported under this section shall report to the Department the information required by the Commission for inclusion in the biological agent registry.

(e) Except as otherwise provided in this section, information prepared for or maintained in the registry under this section shall be confidential and shall not be a public record under G.S. 132-1. The Department may, in accordance with rules adopted by the Commission, release information contained in the biological agent registry for the purpose of conducting or aiding in a communicable disease investigation. The Department shall cooperate with and may share information contained in the biological agent registry with the United States Centers for Disease Control and Prevention, and state and federal law enforcement agencies in any investigation involving the release, theft, or loss of a biological agent required to be reported under this section. Release of information from the registry as authorized under this subsection shall not render the information released a public record under G.S. 132-1. Release of information from the registry as authorized under this subsection also shall not render the information prepared for or maintained in the registry a public record under G.S. 132-1.

(f) The Department shall impose a civil penalty for a willful or knowing violation of this section in the amount of up to one thousand dollars ($1,000). Each day of a continuing violation shall be a separate offense. Any person wishing to contest a penalty shall be entitled to an administrative hearing in accordance with Chapter 150B of the General Statutes.

§ 130A-480. Emergency department data reporting.

(a) For the purpose of ensuring the protection of the public health, the State Health Director shall develop a syndromic surveillance program for hospital emergency departments in order to detect and investigate public health threats that may result from (i) a terrorist incident using nuclear, biological, or chemical agents or (ii) an epidemic or infectious, communicable, or other disease. The State Health Director shall specify the data to be reported by hospitals pursuant to this program, subject to the following:

(1) Each hospital shall submit electronically available emergency department data as specified by rule by the Commission. The Commission, in consultation with hospitals, shall establish by rule a schedule for the implementation of full electronic reporting capability of all data elements by all hospitals. The schedule shall take into consideration the number of data elements already reported by the hospital, the hospital's capacity to electronically maintain the remaining elements, available funding, and other relevant factors.

(2) None of the following data for patients or their relatives, employers, or household members may be collected by the State Health Director: names; postal or street address information, other than town or city, county, state, and the first five digits of the zip code; geocode information; telephone numbers; fax numbers; electronic mail addresses; social security numbers; health plan beneficiary numbers; account

numbers; certificate or license numbers; vehicle identifiers and serial numbers, including license plate numbers; device identifiers and serial numbers; web universal resource locators (URLs); Internet protocol (IP) address numbers; biometric identifiers, including finger and voice prints; and full face photographic images and any comparable images.

(b) The following are not public records under Chapter 132 of the General Statutes and are privileged and confidential:

(1) Data reported to the State Health Director pursuant to this section.

(2) Data collected or maintained by any entity with whom the State Health Director contracts for the reporting, collection, or analysis of data pursuant to this section.

The State Health Director shall maintain the confidentiality of the data reported pursuant to this section and shall ensure that adequate measures are taken to provide system security for all data and information. The State Health Director may share data with local health departments and the Centers for Disease Control and Prevention (CDC) for public health purposes. Local health departments are bound by the confidentiality provisions of this section. The Department shall enter into an agreement with the CDC to ensure that the CDC complies with the confidentiality provisions of this section. The State Health Director shall not allow information that it receives pursuant to this section to be used for commercial purposes and shall not release data except as authorized by other provisions of law.

(c) A person is immune from liability for actions arising from the required submission of data under this Article.

(d) For purposes of this section, "hospital" means a hospital, as defined in G.S. 131E-214.1(3), that operates an emergency room on a 24-hour basis. The term does not include a psychiatric hospital that operates an emergency room.

(e) Administrative emergency department data shall be reported by hospitals under Article 11A of Chapter 131E of the General Statutes.

§ 130A-481. Food defense.

The Department of Agriculture and Consumer Services, Department of Environmental Quality, and Department of Health and Human Services shall jointly develop a plan to protect the food supply from intentional contamination. The plan shall address protection of the food supply from production to consumption, including, but not limited to, the protection of plants, crops, and livestock.

§ 130A-482. Reserved for future codification purposes.

§ 130A-483. Reserved for future codification purposes.

§ 130A-484. Reserved for future codification purposes.

§ 130A-485. Vaccination program established; definitions.

(a) The Department and local health departments shall offer a vaccination program for first responders who may be exposed to infectious diseases when deployed to disaster locations. The vaccinations shall include, but are not limited to, hepatitis A vaccination, hepatitis B vaccination, diphtheria-tetanus vaccination, influenza vaccination, pneumococcal vaccination, and other vaccinations when recommended by the United States Public Health Service and in accordance with Federal Emergency Management Directors Policy. Immune globulin will be made available when necessary, as determined by the State Health Director.

(b) Participation in the vaccination program is voluntary by the first responders, except for first responders who are classified as having "occupational exposure" to bloodborne pathogens as defined by the Occupational Safety and Health Administration Standard contained at 29 C.F.R. § 1910.10300 who shall be required to take the designated vaccinations or otherwise required by law.

(c) Nothing in this section shall require first responders, except first responders for whom the vaccination program is not voluntary as set forth in subsection (b) of this section, who present a written statement from a licensed physician indicating that a vaccine is medically contraindicated for the first responder or who sign a written statement that the administration of a vaccination conflicts with the first responder's religious tenets, to receive a vaccine.

(d) In the event of a vaccine shortage, the State Public Health Director, in consultation with the Centers for Disease Control and Prevention, shall give priority for vaccination to first responders deployed to a disaster location.

(e) The Department shall notify first responders of the availability of the vaccination program and shall provide educational materials on ways to prevent exposure to infectious diseases.

(f) As used in this section, unless the context clearly requires otherwise, the term:

(1) "Bioterrorism" means the intentional use of any microorganism, virus, infectious substance, biological product, or biological agent as defined in G.S. 130A-479 that may be engineered as a result of biotechnology or any naturally occurring or bioengineered component of any microorganism, virus, infectious substance, or biological product to cause or attempt to cause death, disease, or other biological malfunction in any living organism.

(2) "Disaster location" means any geographical location where a bioterrorism attack, terrorist incident, catastrophic or natural disaster, or emergency occurs.

(3) "First responders" means State and local law enforcement personnel, fire department personnel, and emergency medical personnel who will be deployed to bioterrorism attacks, terrorist attacks, catastrophic or natural disasters, or emergencies.

§§ 130A-486 through 130A-490. Reserved for future codification purposes.

Appendix 4

Selected Internet Sites Addressing Communicable Disease Control

University of North Carolina Resources

UNC School of Government North Carolina Public Health Law Microsite
ncphlaw.unc.edu
The North Carolina Public Health Law microsite contains legal information by topic (including communicable disease control law), legislative updates, and information about North Carolina-specific public health law training opportunities. It was designed for people who work with the North Carolina public health system, but it is publicly available for anyone seeking information about North Carolina public health law.

Coates' Canons Local Government Law Blog
http://canons.sog.unc.edu/
More than a dozen faculty members contribute to the School of Government's local government law blog, which is updated two to three times weekly with posts on various legal issues of interest to local government. Posts about communicable disease law can be found by using a keyword search or clicking on the public health topic link.

North Carolina Institute for Public Health (NCIPH) Training Website
https://nciph.sph.unc.edu/tws/index.php
NCIPH is part of the UNC Gillings School of Global Public Health. Its training website offers several brief modules about topics in public health, including modules addressing infectious disease epidemiology, public health preparedness, and communicable disease law.

North Carolina Government Resources

NC Division of Public Health, Epidemiology Section, Communicable Disease Branch

http://epi.publichealth.nc.gov/cd/

This website includes information and North Carolina-specific data about communicable diseases, as well as the activities of the state communicable disease branch and local health departments. It also includes links to the state's communicable disease manuals and to related programs, such as the state laboratory of public health.

Direct link to NC communicable disease manuals: http://epi.public health.nc.gov/cd/lhds/manuals/cd/toc.html.

North Carolina General Assembly

www.ncleg.net

Information about proposed and enacted North Carolina legislation can be found on this site, along with an unofficial version of the state statutes.

Direct link to the North Carolina General Statutes:

www.ncleg.net/gascripts/statutes/Statutes.asp

North Carolina Administrative Code

http://reports.oah.state.nc.us/ncac.asp

The North Carolina Administrative Code compiles the state's administrative rules. Most of the state's communicable disease rules may be found in Title 10A, Chapter 41, Subchapter A.

Federal Government Resources

Centers for Disease Control and Prevention (CDC)

www.cdc.gov

The CDC is the federal government agency that is responsible for tracking, investigating, and researching public health issues and trends. It is part of the U.S. Department of Health and Human Services. The agency's website has detailed information about diseases and conditions, including the guidance documents and recommended actions that form the basis for required communicable disease control measures in North Carolina.

CDC Public Health Law Program
https://www.cdc.gov/phlp/
The CDC Public Health Law Program website has publications and other resources for public health practitioners and their attorneys.

Occupational Safety and Health Administration (OSHA), Bloodborne Pathogens and Needlestick Prevention
https://www.osha.gov/SLTC/bloodbornepathogens/
This website provides guidance documents, FAQs, and other information from OSHA about bloodborne pathogens and the associated federal rules.

Other Resources

Association of State and Territorial Health Officers (ASTHO)
www.astho.org/
ASTHO is a nonprofit organization that represents and serves U.S. state and territorial public health agencies and their employees. It has a program on infectious disease that provides resources and information on public health infrastructure for disease control, as well as other more specific topics.

Direct link to the infectious disease program:
www.astho.org/Programs/Infectious-Disease/

Council of State and Territorial Epidemiologists (CSTE)
CSTE is a professional organization devoted to advancing public health policy and epidemiologic capacity. It has an infectious disease steering committee that works to facilitate prevention, detection, investigation, and control of infectious diseases.
Direct link to the infectious disease task force's information and resources:
http://www.cste.org/group/IDOV

National Association of County and City Health Officials (NACCHO)
www.naccho.org/
NACCHO's members come from local health departments across the United States. The organization promotes public health while adhering to a set of core values, including equity, excellence, leadership, and science.

Its website includes a "toolbox" with information and resources in a number of public health areas, plus a model practices database.

Network for Public Health Law

https://www.networkforphl.org/

The Network for Public Health Law is made up of public health practitioners and attorneys. Its website contains legal information and policy resources. Information that is relevant to communicable disease control is included in the topic of emergency legal preparedness and response.

CPSIA information can be obtained
at www.ICGtesting.com
Printed in the USA
LVOW10s1459280318
571472LV00014B/230/P

9 781560 118794